POTTER'S
WORKSHOP

POTTER'S
WORKSHOP

20 UNIQUE CERAMIC PROJECTS FOR THE SMALL HOME STUDIO

Jenny Rodwell
Photographs by Ian Howes

David & Charles

A DAVID & CHARLES BOOK

First published in the UK in 1999

A catalogue record for this book is available from the British Library.

ISBN 0 7153 0928 5

DESIGNED BY Sue Michniewicz
PHOTOGRAPHY BY Ian Howes

Printed in France by Pollina

for David & Charles
Brunel House
Newton Abbot
Devon

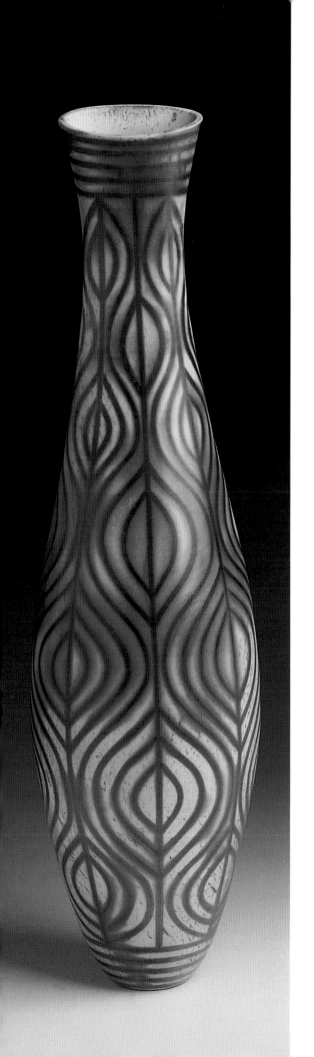

contents

introduction

'Like making the stones under one's feet' is how Sarah Perry, one of the contributors to this book, describes her work. This particular artist makes finely turned bowls and delicate porcelain jewellery, but it is easy to understand what she means about pottery, especially as many early examples *were* the stones underfoot – or at least the sun-baked clay and straw bricks used for paving and building in ancient Egypt.

For something so closely akin to mud, clay has played rather an important role in the history of humankind: not only in the production of bricks for building and pots for cooking, but also in the making and decorating of some very extraordinary and beautiful objects. Not only did the ancient Egyptians, for example, manufacture useful items such as building bricks, but they were also responsible for one of the first known glazes – a soft green developed from steatite, or soapstone – with which they decorated ornamental clay beads. This was a forerunner of the coloured earthenware glazes in use today.

POTTERY OR CERAMICS?

In contemporary ceramics, too, the functional and non-functional aspects continue to flourish – usually side by side, sometimes overlapping, and occasionally at odds with one another. For example, there is currently an ongoing dialogue about the role of pottery, about whether it is an art or a craft, or indeed whether it should be called 'pottery' at all. Some feel the very word suggests a particular sort of ware – chunky, functional, wheel-thrown, or even folksy. For this reason, the term 'ceramics' is preferred by some, with themselves being 'ceramicists' or 'makers' rather than 'potters'.

CLAY: AN ADDICTIVE SUBSTANCE

Whether potter or ceramicist, artist or artisan, the common factor is the clay itself. This may be anything from super-fine bone china with a silky finish to industrial crank, as coarse and gritty as river sand. Whatever your preference, clay is compulsive stuff, and potters have been known to complain of withdrawal symptoms when parted from it for too long. So, to the cautiously interested and the otherwise uninitiated, the message is: once you start, be prepared to get 'hooked'!

TIME AND SPACE

On the other hand, ceramics need not take over your *entire* life and living space. The projects demonstrated in this book actually required very little room and most were not time-consuming to make. Each piece was constructed and decorated on a tabletop, and each is designed to fit into a small electric kiln.

However, the final firings of the raku and smoke-fired pieces must take place out of doors. Although this, too, can be done in a small space, the burning sawdust involved in both types of firing inevitably creates smoke, so you will need the goodwill of any near neighbours. Better still, invite them in to watch, and hope they become converted! After all, raku firings were sometimes a feature of social gatherings in Japan, where the technique was first developed. On arrival at a garden party, each guest would be presented with a biscuit-fired tea bowl and then invited to decorate it using the coloured glazes and brushes provided. The pots were then fired on the spot, each guest being presented with their own decorated bowl.

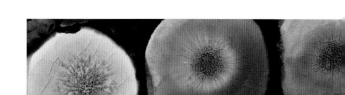

HAND-BUILDING

This book is concerned with hand-building, including coiling, modelling, slab work and pinch pots. The work in it is stylish and contemporary, despite the fact that all the making methods have been in use for as long as people have been digging clay from the ground.

Yet many still associate pottery with thrown vessels and other work done on the wheel. Although it is just as creative as hand-building, throwing pots on the wheel calls for a very different approach. The form and character of a wheel-thrown pot are determined by the method of production, and this is true even when the thrown pot is subsequently altered and modified by the potter, as many are. Hand-building, on the other hand, has few constraints. Provided that the work is soundly constructed and will fit into your kiln, there are no restrictions on size and shape.

Another great difference between throwing and hand-building is the speed with which the work is done. On a wheel, hundreds of pots can be made in a comparatively short period of time. With hand-building, even though pots are sometimes produced in runs or series, the process usually takes longer. The very nature of hand-building makes it a slower, more contemplative process.

ABOUT THIS BOOK

The first part of *Potter's Workshop* is about materials and tools. It includes an introduction to clays and glazes, and the tools and equipment needed to use them.

The second part shows how pots and ceramic pieces are made. The contributors to this section are all experts in their own field. Between them, they cover an extremely broad spectrum of ceramic design, materials and techniques. Their work includes jewellery, garden sculpture, modelling, earthenware, stoneware, tiles, raku and smoke firing.

As well as giving a fascinating insight into their art, the contributors also provide a wealth of practical information and the benefit of their unique experience and professional expertise. Each illustrated demonstration shows a personal approach – one artist's way of working. However, clay is a tactile medium and pictures can only show so much. The most effective and enjoyable way to learn about pottery is with hands-on experience – by getting your own hands dirty and having a go.

It is hoped that this book will provide you with inspiration, a starting point for your own ideas, and that you will then go on to develop a personal approach, using original designs and techniques. *Potter's Workshop* aims to help and encourage.

STUDIO PRACTICE

Finally, a word about health and safety. Like many activities, pottery involves using materials which can be dangerous if not handled properly. Some are poisonous if taken by mouth, others are damaging if inhaled or absorbed through the skin. General advice about safe studio practice is given on pages 140–141, and in addition it is important to follow the manufacturer's instructions when using any product.

However, it is also essential to enjoy what you are doing without becoming over-anxious, so a sense of perspective is required. Take proper precautions, and pottery is as safe as any other activity.

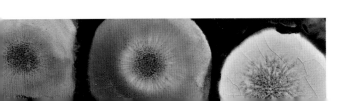

the basics

This part of the book is a general introduction to clays, glazes and other ceramic materials. It also contains illustrated advice on basic techniques, such as preparing clay, mixing and applying glazes, and other elementary procedures.

In addition to practical advice, there are also gallery pages. These feature various types of ceramic ware and also show examples of pots decorated in different ways – with glazes, oxides and coloured slips.

BUYING MATERIALS

The majority of professional potters actually use very few materials. Having discovered their preferred area, they tend to use the same clay and perhaps a handful of glazes for all their work. For the experienced potter this is all very well, but for the newcomer it is a good idea to try out various different techniques, and this means buying a few basic materials.

Fortunately, many manufactures recognize this need and most of the materials mentioned in this section can be purchased in small amounts. Even clay can often be obtained in trial packs.

CLAYS

Clay and most other materials used in pottery come from the ground. Many potters enjoy digging and using their own local clay, and a large part of their work satisfaction comes from that part of the process.

Buying clay often means choosing from a great many different types, all pre-packed in plastic bags. It is easy to forget the origins of the substance and to feel overawed by choice and packaging. For the beginner, it is important to remember that what you are buying is mud from the ground. The manufacturer has done the hard work – found the clay, dug it up and packed it. Sometimes two or more clays are combined to give a better product; sometimes various materials are added to alter its texture

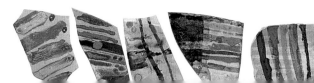

and properties, to make the clay more stable at certain temperatures and more suitable for specific types of work.

In fact, the manufacturer has simply improved the product and made sure you get exactly the same quality each time you buy a pack of clay. Take advantage of the trial packs to try out a number of clay bodies to see which you like best.

THE SCIENCE OF POTTERY

Ceramics works on many levels. Some potters are extremely knowledgeable about the chemistry of glazes and clay – about which ingredients do what, and why; some have learned enough chemistry for their needs; others have no scientific background but have nevertheless built up a store of practical knowledge simply by trial and error.

The following pages outline the main types of glaze and how they are used, in general rather than scientific terms. However, whether you are a scientist or not, all glaze recipes should be tested. This applies even to recipes from reputable sources. There are lots of variables in ceramics; no two kilns are alike, and no two firing conditions are the same.

It is essential to keep a record of your glaze trials – of the ingredients, the thickness of the glaze, the clay body and the firing times. This way, when you turn up a glaze you really like, you have a good chance of getting the same result again.

TOOLS AND EQUIPMENT

The proper tools make any job easier, and the main items are covered in this section. Investing in a few pieces of quality equipment is always a good idea. However, there is nothing to stop you from improvising some of your own. Cut-up credit cards for scraping and shaping, bent kitchen cutlery for modelling and burnishing, hair combs and toothbrushes for texturing – so many innovative tools can make useful additions to the studio tool box.

WHAT IS CLAY?

Clay comes from granite and other rocks which have been gradually weathered by water and heat, wind and frost. It takes literally millions of years for the clay to form, and even then it is rarely absolutely right for the potter to use without first making a few alterations and additions.

Clays can be divided into two main groups: primary and secondary. Primary clay has formed over millions of years in the same place and is found on the site of its formation. As a general rule, primary clays – the best known of which is china clay – are free from impurities, and are light or white in colour. They also tend to be non-plastic (see below), and therefore difficult for the potter to use in their natural state.

A secondary clay, on the other hand, has been carried by water, glaciers, shifting earth, and even wind. During its travels, the clay has picked up impurities which affect its colour and character. For example, red clays contain iron, and ball clays contain carbons which make them grey or bluish-black in their unfired state. So much movement and weathering has broken down the particles of the clay that it is much more workable, or 'plastic', than primary clay.

BOUGHT CLAYS Although some potters like to dig and prepare their own clay, most are happy to walk into a pottery supply shop and buy the clay of their choice, pre-packed and ready to use. These bought clays are made from different types of natural clay blended together to get the best of the individual properties – good plasticity, low shrinkage and so on. Sand, quartz, iron compounds or other minerals are sometimes added to improve the clay or to achieve a specific characteristic. The projects in this book are all made with bought clays.

The simplest and most popular supplied clay comes in 'plastic' form – it is wet and can be used straight from the pack. It is generally packed in strong polythene bags which, if properly stored, will retain their condition for many months. Alternatively, some clays are available in powder form and these must be mixed with water and prepared before use.

TEXTURE As a general rule, a coarsely textured clay holds its shape and is best for modelling and hand-building. A very smooth clay is usually better for throwing, as it may be too floppy for hand-building.

Coarseness is usually introduced in the form of 'grog' – gritty particles made from ground fired clay, ground firebricks or other refractory material. The introduction of grog into a clay body also increases firing strength and reduces the rate of shrinkage of the clay during drying and firing. Molochite is ground fired china clay, and its whiteness makes it suitable for use as a grog in porcelain and other white clays.

Your supplier will tell you which clays are grogged and which are not. Very coarsely grogged clays create a rough-textured surface which makes them unsuitable for fine or detailed work, but they have good resistance to warping and cracking.

Clay textures Clay comes in all textures, depending on the amount of grog – gritty particles – in the clay body. The samples here are smooth (1), medium grogged (2), coarse (3), and slightly grogged (4).

Powder clays Many clays can be bought in powder form and used in plastic clay, slips and glazes. The samples here are chocolate black (1), buff stoneware (2), ball clay (3), and china clay (4).

COLOUR Natural clays vary in colour from white and off-white, through buff, to red, brown and black. In addition, you can make variously coloured clay bodies by adding commercial stains to powdered clay prior to mixing (see pages 28–29).

CLAY TYPES Clays are usually categorized according to their firing temperature or their suitability for a particular type of ware or technique.

Earthenware is the most universally common clay body, with a firing temperature of 1000°–1180°C. Most suppliers offer a range of smooth and grogged earthenware in reds, whites and off-whites, as well as a brownish-black. **Stoneware** is usually fired to 1200°–1300°C, occasionally higher. A fired stoneware body is dense, glass-like and generally impermeable, especially when fired to the higher temperatures. Colours normally range from white to buff. **Porcelain** requires a high firing temperature of 1220°–1350°C, depending on the type. It is hard and very white. If used thinly, many porcelain clay bodies are translucent when fired. **Bone china**, so-called because the clay body contains about 50 per cent calcined bone, is popular for its whiteness and combined delicacy and toughness. Having a non-plastic nature, bone china is usually used for slip-casting rather than modelling or hand-building. **T-material** is very resilient and warp resistant, with very little thermal expansion. It is one of the 'safest' clays, especially for firing techniques which involve sudden changes of temperature.

Grogs Grogs are graded according to the size of the particles, which are graded from dust to 3mm and larger. The samples are 0.2mm to dust (1), 0.4–0.2mm (2) 3mm to dust (3), and 1.5–0.8mm (4).

Clay types Ten popular clay bodies are shown here in their leather-hard form (right-hand column) and fired state (left-hand column). The samples demonstrate the degree of shrinkage that takes place during drying and firing.

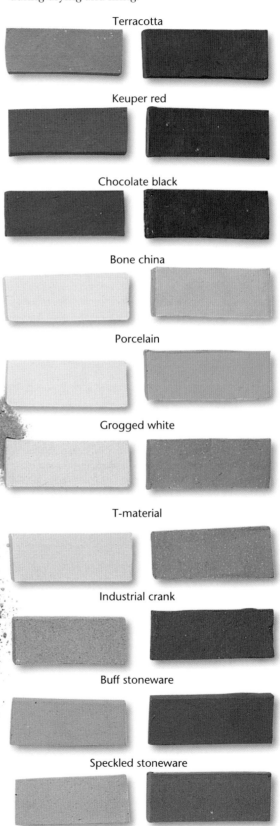

Terracotta

Keuper red

Chocolate black

Bone china

Porcelain

Grogged white

T-material

Industrial crank

Buff stoneware

Speckled stoneware

PREPARING CLAY

Clay must have a completely even consistency before it can be used. Even a newly bought bag of ready-to-use clay will probably have been lying around the factory or shop for some time; it may have settled unevenly, or the outer clay will have dried out more than clay at the centre of the pack. In any event, 'wedging' and 'kneading' are the two methods used to get rid of unevenness, lumps and trapped air in plastic clay.

WEDGING This technique is used to produce an even consistency in the clay, and also for blending two or more different clays together. There are various ways of wedging, but a traditional method is to cut the clay in two, turn the top piece around and then slam it down on the bottom piece, repeating the process until the clay is evenly mixed and there is no sign of air bubbles.

KNEADING Similar to kneading bread or pastry, the wedged clay is now given a final mix by being cut into balls of a manageable size and kneaded until the texture and consistency are uniform throughout. This method is known as 'sheep's-head' or 'bull's-head' kneading, because the kneaded clay resembles the head of an animal.

An alternative method, especially good for larger quantities of clay, is known as 'spiral' kneading or wedging, so-called because the worked clay eventually forms a shell-like spiral. The approach is similar to the sheep's-head method, but here the pressure is applied to one side of the clay only. With practice, a regular rocking motion develops which manipulates the clay into a uniform consistency.

ROLLING When the clay has been thoroughly prepared, it is ready for use. For many hand-building techniques, the clay must first be made into a flat slab. This is usually done with a rolling pin on a wooden surface, taking care that the clay does not stick. Some potters like to roll on a piece of hessian or cloth so that the rolled piece can be turned and handled easily.

RECLAIMING Clay need never be wasted. Provided it has not become contaminated or mixed with other types of clay, all unfired clay can be recycled and used again. It is especially important not to mix stoneware clay with earthenware clay. Apart from causing discoloration, earthenware clay may blister when fired to stoneware temperatures. Use different containers for each type of clay, and cover the clay while soaking to prevent dust and particles falling in.

Left-over clay can be soaked in water to break down the large lumps and then spread on a plaster of Paris slab to absorb excess moisture. (See page 140 for advice on how to make a plaster slab.) When the clay is dry enough to handle it can be lifted easily from the slab, before being wedged and kneaded in the normal way.

STORAGE Clay actually improves with age, so recycled and wedged clay can be stored for some time. The polythene bags in which the clay was delivered are ideal for storing prepared clay, provided dry flakes on the inside of the bags are first damped down with a sponge.

Alternatively, use bin liners, plastic sacks or plastic carrier bags. Bags should be well sealed and stored in a cool, frost-free place, away from direct sunlight.

Similarly, a piece of unfinished work can be wrapped in plastic sheeting or cling film overnight or longer, to prevent the clay drying out and making further work impossible. Avoid placing unfinished work on plaster or wood, as these surfaces are porous and will absorb moisture from the clay, causing it to dry unevenly.

WEDGING

1 Take a piece of clay and cut it in two by slicing it with a cutting wire.

2 Lift the top piece of clay and turn it through an angle of approximately 90 degrees.

3 Slam the top half down on the bottom half. Turn the whole piece towards you through 90 degrees and repeat the process until the clay is evenly wedged.

'SHEEP'S HEAD' KNEADING

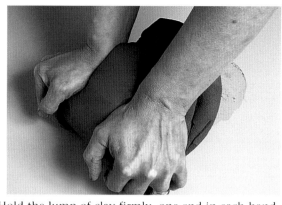

1 Hold the lump of clay firmly, one end in each hand, and simultaneously press downwards and outwards, spreading the clay with your palms.

2 Lift and tilt the 'forehead' slightly towards you so that the tip of the 'chin' is on the tabletop, and then repeat the process until the clay is evenly kneaded.

SPIRAL KNEADING

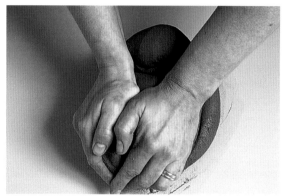

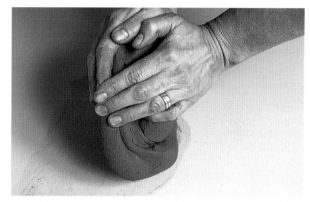

1 To knead a large lump of clay, start by pressing with both hands on one corner of the clay, pressing downwards and outwards at the same time.

2 Lift the clay and bring it back into the same position on the tabletop, holding the top of the clay with both your hands.

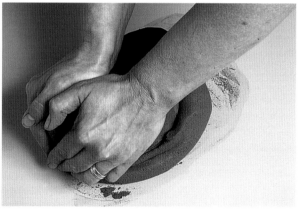

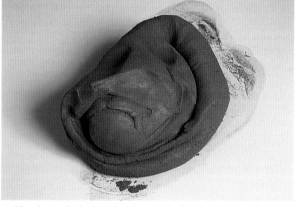

3 Repeat the kneading process, pressing down with both hands on the same corner of the clay and again pressing downwards and outwards.

4 The kneaded clay forms a spiral, which can then be worked into a more uniform shape by rolling and shaping it on the table.

ROLLING

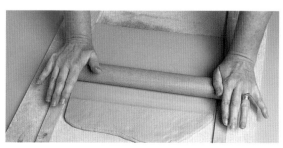

To obtain a slab of clay of even thickness, roll it between two wooden guides of the thickness that you want the clay. Continue until you are rolling on the guides. Both the rolling pin and the tabletop must be absolutely dry. For a thin sheet of clay, or if the slab is to be moved and handled, roll on a piece of hessian or cloth.

UNGLAZED
A Mochica-ware
bird jug from South
America, c500AD. The figure is painted with
several layers of slip stained with animal or
vegetable matter, before being burnished and
then fired in an open oven. This is probably a
ritualistic funeral piece, made for burial with
the body.

STONEWARE
Glazed pot by Reginald Wells of the Coldrum Pottery,
Chelsea, c1910–1914. Wells was one of the earliest
studio potters and was particularly interested in
Chinese glazing techniques. This pot is decorated in
typically subtle and delicate colours, using poured red
and green glazes.

PRESS-MOULDED
WHITE EARTHENWARE
A Staffordshire dog c1850, one of
many animal figures produced in that
county during the nineteenth
century. The model is press
moulded and decorated with
on-glaze colours.

SMOKE FIRED

A twentieth-century smoke-decorated earthenware vessel by Janet Leach. Formerly Janet Darnell, the third wife of Bernard Leach was also a potter and ran the Leach pottery in St Ives until 1983. This pot is formed in red earthenware clay and decorated with heavily carbonized smoke-fired markings.

EARTHENWARE

A coarse earthenware vessel made in Yorkshire, probably in the eighteenth century. The inside and top half are dipped in an iron glaze – dipped earthenware vessels such as this were common in every home at that time. The lead glaze used on this pot is now illegal, but domestic earthenware pots of similar size and shape are still being made today.

TOOLS

TOOLS FOR MAKING There is such a wide selection of excellent tools available to the contemporary potter that decisions can be difficult. For the newcomer to pottery, who wants to experiment and try different materials and techniques, it is tempting to go out and spend a fortune on tools, each designed for a particular job. As a rule of thumb, it is a good idea to start with just a few basic tools, adding to these as your needs increase.

Interestingly, many professional potters have surprisingly little equipment. Having developed a particular way of working, they tend to stick to a few favourite tools, which are often used for many years.

A selection of tools specially made for hand-building is shown here.

1 Rubber kidney made from flexible rubber, for smoothing plastic clay surfaces.
2 Serrated kidney, for rapid smoothing and texturing of leather-hard clay.
3 Smooth kidney, used mainly for trimming leather-hard clay.
4 Bow harp, which enables a stack of slabs to be cut from a single block of clay.
5 Variously shaped boxwood modelling tools, used for modelling and decorating clay in its plastic state.
6 Variously shaped wire modelling tools, used for cutting, fluting and hollowing soft clay.
7 Double-ended steel modelling tools, used for shaping and carving clay or plaster surfaces.
8 Bow trimmer, used for trimming clay, especially in pressed and slab work.
9 Coiler, used for producing coils quickly and easily.
10 General-purpose potter's knife for cutting, fettling and trimming.
11 Hole cutter, used for making holes in lamp bases, teapots etc. The blade is half-round to prevent clogging.
12 Wire cutter, for cutting blocks of clay.
13 Wooden sieves with stainless steel mesh, for sieving glazes and slips.
14 Small sieve ('cup lawn'), useful for small quantities of colour and test glazes.

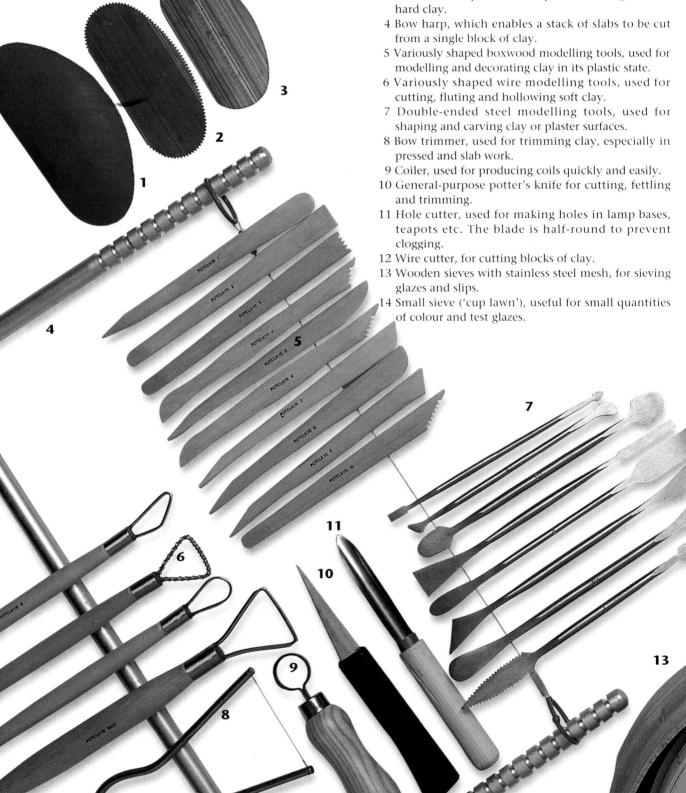

TOOLS FOR DECORATING Traditional decorative techniques are done with glazes, slips and oxides. For these you will need a selection of brushes, including large soft ones for applying colour to wide areas, and smaller artist's brushes for detailed work. Again, one or two quality brushes are a good starting point and will last for years if well cared for.

Tools for making incised and textured decoration vary enormously, depending on the effect required. Apart from the items shown here, other useful pieces of equipment can often be found around the home. For example, a table fork, a knitting needle and a teaspoon are among the improvised tools used on the projects in this book.

15 Variously shaped carved printing sticks, which make a distinct mark when pressed into clay or when applying slip.
16 Ceramic decorator's palette, useful for mixing pigments, oxides and other decorating materials.
17 Potter's pens, which contain ready-mixed under-glaze colours and are used mainly for linear patterns, lettering and drawing.
18 Slip trailer, a rounded rubber bulb used for slip decoration. The detachable nozzle is cut to the required hole size.
19 Underglaze pencils, for fine line shading, script and other linear decoration.
20 Kazan brush.
21 Glaze mop.
22 Japanese brush.
23 Rigger brush.

24 Flat hake brush.
25 Clay shapers, with soft chisel edges that can be used to create distinctive 'brush' strokes with decorative pigments.
26 Natural sponges.

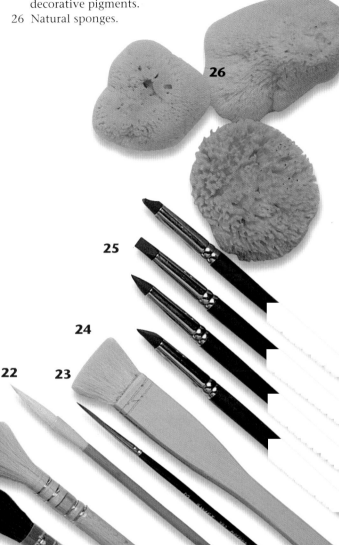

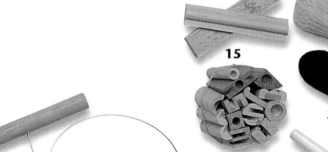

GLAZING

The earliest glazes were purely functional, developed and used to make porous clay pots watertight. Although still essential for table- and ovenware, glazes have become increasingly complex and decorative. To many contemporary potters, the aesthetic and functional reasons for glazing are of equal importance.

A glaze is simply a layer of thin glass fused on to the surface of the pot. Each glaze is specially formulated to match a particular type of clay and firing method. In other words, the clay and the glaze must mature at approximately the same temperature.

The glaze must also 'fit' the clay body – the glaze and clay must expand and shrink at approximately the same rate during firing and cooling. A poor glaze 'fit' produces disappointing results, including 'crazing', when the glaze has an overall pattern of fine cracks, and 'crawling', which results in bare patches and puckering on the glaze surface.

BISCUIT AND RAW GLAZING Most glazes are applied to a pot which has already been fired to a fairly low temperature, usually somewhere between 950°C and 1000°C. This preliminary firing is known as a 'biscuit' or 'bisque' firing. and pots which have been fired in this way are usually referred to as biscuit- or bisque-ware. The higher the biscuit firing, the more vitreous and dense the pot, and the more difficult it may be to apply glaze. However, a high biscuit firing will often help to avoid crazing and other glaze problems which occasionally crop up with earthenware glazes.

Some potters skip the biscuit firing, preferring instead to 'once fire' or 'green glaze' their work – that is, the glaze is applied to the leather-hard pot, allowed to dry, and then fired to the desired temperature. Once firing is more risky than biscuit firing, partly because the unfired body can collapse or blister under the application of wet glaze, especially if the clay has become too dry. The firing itself must be slow and steady to allow moisture to escape from the clay through the glaze.

WHAT'S IN A GLAZE? Most glaze recipes include three basic ingredients – silica, alumina and a flux. The latter is also known as the 'base'. The proportion and nature of these three main ingredients determines the nature of the glaze and the temperature at which it melts and matures. The silica is the 'glass'-forming ingredient; the flux controls the melting and spreading; and the

alumina contributes to the hardness and stability of the glaze. In addition to these basic ingredients, a glaze recipe may contain various added ingredients in order to determine or modify the nature of the finished glaze, including its colour, texture and opacity.

Glazes are coloured with metallic oxides, commercially prepared stains or a combination of both (see pages 26–29).

EARTHENWARE AND STONEWARE GLAZES

Earthenware glazes, or 'soft' glazes as they are sometimes called, are typically smooth and shiny. Stoneware glazes, on the other hand, are seldom shiny; because of their higher firing temperature, they tend to be matt or satiny in appearance.

The difference between the two glazes lies in the flux. In earthenware glazes the main flux is normally lead or

Stoneware glaze tests Sample glaze tests, showing the effects of combined and overlaid stoneware colours. The tests are done on pieces of broken biscuit-ware.

Stoneware test tiles Test tiles showing five basic translucent or semi-transparent stoneware glazes.
1 Potash feldspar 60 parts; quartz 40 parts; whiting 20 parts.
2 Potash feldspar 50 parts; whiting 40 parts; china clay 20 parts.
3 Potash feldspar 25 parts; china clay 25 parts; whiting 25 parts; quartz 25 parts.
4 Potash feldspar 40 parts; dolomite 30 parts; china clay 20 parts; flint 10 parts.
5 Cornish stone 50 parts; dolomite 22 parts; china clay 24 parts; whiting 4 parts.

1   2   3   4   5

borax, whereas stoneware glazes are usually based on feldspar or wood ash. Earthenware glazes are fired to between 950°C and 1180°C; glazes fired to over 1200°C are usually classified as stoneware glazes.

OXIDIZED AND REDUCTION FIRINGS The atmosphere in the kiln dictates the appearance of the finished glaze. In an electric kiln, as used in the projects in this book, the kiln atmosphere is 'oxidized' – that is, there is plenty of oxygen to combine with the metal in the glaze and clay during firing.

In a 'reduction' firing the oxygen supply is reduced or controlled, causing the metals to react differently, and often unpredictably. For instance, a copper glaze may produce a range of colours including reds and purples, whereas in an oxidized firing it will usually be green or turquoise. Reduction firing is usually done in a gas kiln, as it tends to ruin the elements in an electric kiln.

GLAZE TESTS Before making up a large batch of any glaze, it is always a good idea to mix and test a small quantity first. Even ready-made, bought glazes can be disappointing and may not be what you had in mind. Most suppliers sell glaze mixtures in small quantities, and a trial run on small items or test tiles can save time and money in the long run.

Earthenware test tiles Test tiles experimenting with overlaid, coloured earthenware glazes. The basic glaze is: lead basilicate 58 parts; standard borax frit 30 parts; potash feldspar 3 parts; china clay 9 parts; Hyplas ball clay 10 parts. Added to this were 5 parts of commercial colouring stain. The tiles were fired to a high earthenware temperature.

BUYING GLAZES

Many glaze ranges can be purchased direct from the supplier. Some come in powder form and are mixed with water and sieved ready for use; others come in liquid or 'slop' form. It is quite common for a potter to buy a good base glaze, either white or transparent, to which colouring oxides and pigments are then added. Glaze ranges vary from one make to another, and it is important to buy your glazes from a reputable manufacturer.

The choice of bought glazes is vast and increasing all the time. As well as a wide range of stoneware and earthenware glazes, there are also many beautiful decorative and 'special effect' glazes on the market.

For the potter with limited space and time, or for those who are not interested in developing their own glaze recipes, there is much to be said for the convenience of bought glazes. Another great advantage is that such glazes have been tested and classified to meet specified safety requirements.

Certain fired colours and glazes may release lead and other metallic compounds when in contact with acidic foods and drinks over a period of time, and this can be a health hazard if the amount released is above a certain level. Your manufacturer or supplier will be able to tell you exactly which glazes are suitable for tableware, which can be used on ovenware, and which are for decorative purposes only.

POWDERED GLAZES Traditionally, bought stoneware, earthenware and raku glazes come in powder form. These can be ordered in any quantity, usually from half a kilo upwards. The more you buy, the lower the price. However, for experimenting and for one-off pieces it is a good idea to start with a small amount until you know whether or not you like the result.

BRUSH-ON AND DECORATIVE GLAZES These easy-to-use glazes come in jars and are usually applied to biscuit-ware. Unusual and distinctive effects can be achieved instantly and easily with many of these glazes. Some of them produce special effects, such as crystal patterns and multicoloured marbling.

Many decorative glaze ranges are completely non-toxic, which makes them particularly suitable for use where there are young children around.

All the glazes shown here are produced and marketed by Potclays Limited.

Earthenware glazes A range of earthenware glazes available in both powder and brush-on form. Depending on the individual glaze, these earthenware colours are fired to between 960°C and 1125°C. The three colours bottom right are for raku firing (see pages 38–39).

Stoneware glazes All the glazes in this range are leadless and pass all known safety statutes. The glaze samples here are fired in an electric kiln at 1230°–1300°C, depending on the colour.

Porcelain glazes A range of glazes made specially for use with porcelain. The firing temperatures are the same as for the stoneware glazes above.

Special glazes Fired in the range 1200°–1260°C, the Mineral range of stoneware glazes are semi-matt, becoming progressively shinier with increasing temperature.

Reactive glazes This particular range of reactive glazes are used as low-temperature stoneware glazes (1180°–1230°C) or as underglazes. When covered with higher-temperature glazes, the two react together during stoneware firing to create a variety of effects.

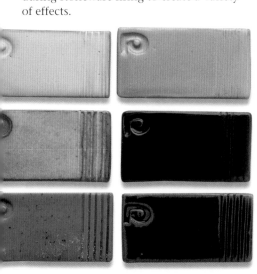

USING GLAZES

How a glaze is applied to a pot depends on the size and shape of the work, and also on the type of surface you want to achieve.

The glazed projects in this book are either dipped, poured or painted. For larger works, or for a more regular finish, glaze can also be sprayed. However, this requires a spray gun and a ventilated spraying booth – a fairly expensive piece of equipment which also requires space for installation.

MIXING A glaze can be mixed by adding the water to the powder, as demonstrated here, or the other way round. Either way, the ratio of water to powder should be in the region of about 1 litre (2 pints) of water to 400g (1lb) of glaze powder. However, too much water is not usually a problem, because after the glaze has been standing for a few hours any excess can be poured off.

Store the mixed glaze in a lidded plastic container and label it immediately with the manufacturer's name and glaze reference number or the recipe, and the firing temperature. It is surprisingly easy to confuse one glaze with another if they are not properly marked.

As with all dry ceramics materials, always wear a mask and plastic or surgical gloves when handling powdered glaze (see pages 140–141).

SETTLING Glazes tend to settle and must be mixed thoroughly before use. Use a rubber glove and stir the mixture, lifting the sediment from the bottom of the bucket with one hand while trying not to disturb the surface of the mixture. This can create air bubbles, which cause tiny pinhole marks in the glaze.

The addition of bentonite to a glaze – normally at a rate of 1–5 per cent of the weight of the dry ingredients – will help avoid the settling problem. You will need to mix the powdered bentonite to a slurry first, before adding it to the glaze slop.

CONSISTENCY The thickness of the glaze should normally be similar to that of thin or thick cream. As a general rule, thinner glazes are for earthenware, very porous biscuit-ware and thick-walled pots; thicker glazes are for stoneware and thin-walled pots. However, it is always a good idea to make tests first to determine the exact results.

MIXING A GLAZE

1 Weigh the dry ingredients into a bowl or bucket.

2 Add the water to the powder (about 1 litre/2 pints water to 400g/1lb glaze, or enough almost to cover it). Stir the mixture and leave it to soak for about half an hour to help break down the lumps.

3 Pass the mixture through a 100 mesh sieve. If this is difficult, pass it through a 60 mesh sieve first and then try again.

4 Use a rubber kidney or stiff brush to rub the mixture through the sieve. Allow the glaze to stand before using, preferably overnight.

DIPPING

1 To glaze a vessel, dip the pot in the glaze as far as possible, making sure the inside is completely covered. Pour the glaze out quickly.

2 If necessary, complete the dipping by carefully submerging any parts that have not been glazed, allowing the glaze just to overlap the already glazed areas. Shake gently from side to side, allowing excess glaze to drip off.

BRUSHING

Glaze can be applied with a very soft brush – a useful technique when there is not enough glaze for dipping. Here even bands of brushed glaze are applied to a plate using a whirler, or banding wheel.

POURING

Large or awkward items which cannot be dipped can be supported over a bucket or bowl and the glaze poured over them. Vessels and pots should be glazed on the inside first.

CLEANING THE BASE

Any glaze on the base of the pot must be removed carefully with a damp sponge or cloth to prevent it sticking to the kiln shelf during firing. An alternative is to coat the base of the pot with wax resist before applying the glaze.

FETTLING

Drips and thick ridges of overlapped glaze can be smoothed carefully by scraping, or 'fettling', with a metal kidney, fettling knife or other suitable tool.

LUSTRE GLAZE

Contemporary thrown stoneware bowls with lustre-decorated rims, by Sarah Perry. The bright blue matt is a copper–barium glaze fired to stoneware temperature. Gold lustre is applied as a separate firing and takes on the matt finish of the underlying barium glaze.

SALT GLAZE

This salt-glazed bottle, made in Germany in the eighteenth century, was manufactured as a container for imported wines. Salt is thrown into the hot kiln to form a characteristically dimpled, tough glaze surface. Nowadays salt glazing is a studio technique, but when this bottle was made such glazes were used mainly on cheap jars and bottles.

RAKU GLAZE

Contemporary raku bowl by Pat Fuller, thrown in red raku clay and altered to create the distinctive, slightly assymetrical shape. The bowl is then dipped in white slip and biscuit fired, before being glazed with a clear raku crackle glaze.

GLAZE OVER REACTIVE SLIP

Small bird bath in Kathmandu pattern, by Karin Hessenberg. The contemporary stoneware bird bath is slab built and decorated with white glaze over a reactive slip, before being fired to 1280°C in an electric kiln. A reactive slip is one which begins to melt before the top glaze, causing the slip to appear through the glaze.

COLOUR:
OXIDES AND NATURAL PIGMENTS

Colours for the potter come in the form of metal oxides and natural pigments, as well as commercially prepared and mixed stains. Both are available in powder form and can be mixed into powdered clay bodies and glaze before adding water. They can also be added to slips, or painted on to biscuit-ware or leather-hard pots. The strength or brightness of an oxide colour depends on the amount used.

When they are used as a painted colour on a pot to be glazed, it is a good idea to mix the oxides with a binder or gum medium such as gum arabic rather than water. This way, the colours are less likely to rub off the pot. It is also advisable to fire the oxides to biscuit temperature before applying the glaze. Apart from preventing the oxides from contaminating the glaze, this also ensures a more even colour.

Great care should be taken when handling all oxides. Although some are more dangerous than others, as a general rule inhaling, taking by mouth and skin contact should be avoided at all times.

OXIDE COLOURS Metal oxides are natural colourants used extensively in ceramics. They are available in prepared powder form and provide a range of colours from earthy reds, yellows, browns and greens through to bright blue, turquoise, purple, grey and black. Rather like the painter's palette, oxides can be mixed and combined to produce an even wider range of effects and colours.

However, when using metal oxides the final colours are determined by the type of firing – whether it is oxidized or reduced. They are also affected by the other ingredients in the glaze. So, although oxides can produce beautiful and harmonious effects, it is not always easy to control the final results, or even to repeat an exact effect.

OXIDES AND COLOURANTS Cobalt is a very stable blue pigment that will produce a range of pale to deep blues depending on the quantity used. Blue glazes usually contain about 2 per cent cobalt or less. Used on its own, cobalt is a strong, sometimes rather harsh colour, and is therefore often modified by mixing with other substances such as iron and red clay. Compared with other oxides, cobalt has a high firing temperature, so firing to biscuit temperature will not necessarily fix the oxide to the pot.

Nickel makes rather dull tones of grey and brown and is therefore not often used as a colouring oxide. However, it is frequently used for toning down and modifying other oxides. Nickel can be unstable at 1200°C and above.

Iron colourings – including red iron oxide, black iron oxide, synthetic iron oxide, crocus martis, iron chromate and others – create a range of earthy hues from brick red through to subtle purples, browns, blacks and greys. The result depends to a large extent on the firing temperature, and on the type of glaze, if used as a glaze colourant.

Copper tends to produce a rather dull brown stain on biscuit-ware, but is capable of producing very bright glazes. As a glaze colourant in oxidized firings, copper will create greens and turquoises; in a reduction firing it can produce reds, purples and other colours. Copper is a powerful colourant, and too much in a glaze will produce a burnt black. It also tends to make a glaze run. The usual amount is under 3 per cent.

Manganese creates pinks, purples, blacks and greys, depending on the temperature to which it is fired. When used with copper, it produces a metallic gold. Manganese is one of the more dangerous oxides and great care should be taken when using it.

Chromium is a standard source of green in pottery, but the colours are opaque and tend to be rather dull. In high firings, it turns yellow. Chromium is toxic and should be used with care and not inhaled.

Vanadium is a rather weak colouring agent, producing yellows and oranges. In glazes it is used in quantities of up to 10 per cent, becoming matt and opaque in high firings. Vanadium can be absorbed through the skin, and should always be handled with gloves.

Rutile has little effective colouring powers of its own, so is used mainly for its effect on other oxides and colourants. It can break up other colours to produce a distinctive mottled effect, particularly in glazes containing borax.

Tin is used mainly as an opacifier and to obtain white glazes at all temperatures. Tin oxide can also have the effect of enhancing and softening other colours.

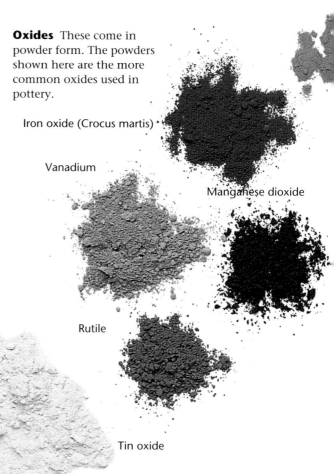

Oxides These come in powder form. The powders shown here are the more common oxides used in pottery.

Iron oxide (Crocus martis)

Vanadium

Manganese dioxide

Rutile

Tin oxide

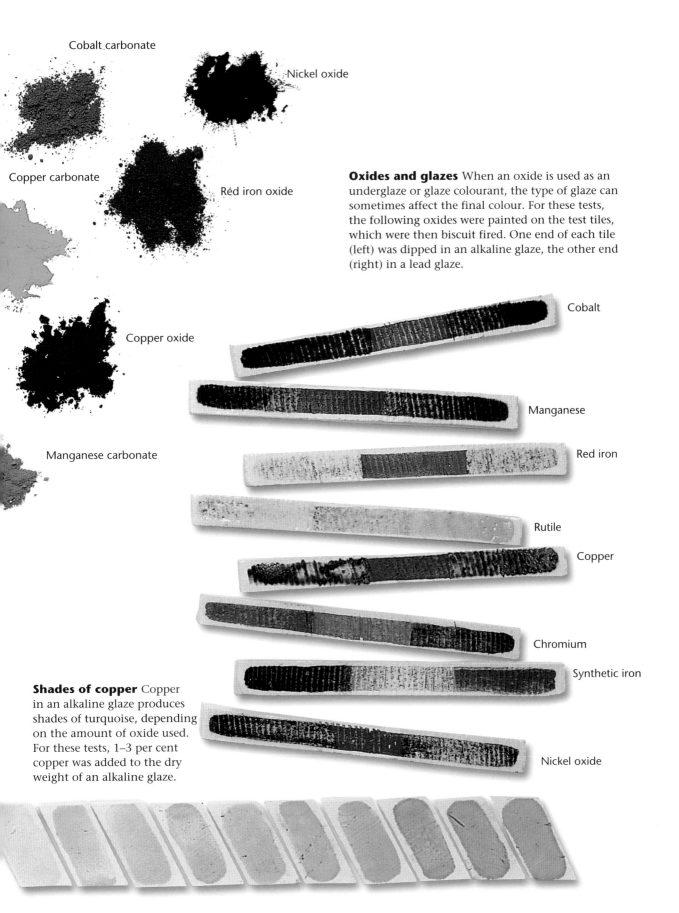

Cobalt carbonate

Nickel oxide

Copper carbonate

Réd iron oxide

Copper oxide

Manganese carbonate

Oxides and glazes When an oxide is used as an underglaze or glaze colourant, the type of glaze can sometimes affect the final colour. For these tests, the following oxides were painted on the test tiles, which were then biscuit fired. One end of each tile (left) was dipped in an alkaline glaze, the other end (right) in a lead glaze.

Cobalt

Manganese

Red iron

Rutile

Copper

Chromium

Synthetic iron

Nickel oxide

Shades of copper Copper in an alkaline glaze produces shades of turquoise, depending on the amount of oxide used. For these tests, 1–3 per cent copper was added to the dry weight of an alkaline glaze.

COLOUR:
CLAY AND GLAZE STAINS

Easier to control than basic metal oxides, commercially prepared stains have been specially formulated and stabilized. Unlike natural oxides, most of these prepared stains do not alter a great deal when fired to the recommended temperature. Although one or two of the colours are slightly different in their fired state, the raw unfired colours are similar enough to the fired colours for you to be able to anticipate the finished result.

Commercial stains come in various forms. Some are made specially for mixing with the clay body or slip, some are for adding to glazes, and some can be used for both. Also available are on-glaze colours for decorating glazed pots, and underglaze colours for decorating pots prior to glazing. The latter are also available in pen and pencil form for calligraphy and making linear designs.

The colour range of all these is extensive, and includes primary red and yellow – neither of which is obtainable from metal oxides.

Body and glaze stains This range of colours can be used either as glaze stains (5–8 per cent of the dry ingredients) or as slip and clay body stains (10–18 per cent of the dry ingredients). The glaze here brings out the intensity of the colours. The stains shown here are produced and marketed by Potclays Limited.

UNDERGLAZE COLOURS In liquid form, underglaze colours have the same consistency as paint and are brushed on to biscuit-ware or unfired clay. There is also a powdered variety, which can be mixed with a binding medium or gum solution and used for painting. Some powdered glaze and body stains can also be used as underglaze painting colours, in the same way.

Underglaze decoration shows through subsequent glaze applications, which should be transparent or white if the colours are not to be affected by the glaze pigment.

Underglaze pencils
For use under a clear glaze, ceramic pencils are good for all linear decoration and for marking pots and test tiles. The pencil cores are made from ceramic materials and break easily, so they must be used carefully.

Unglazed body stains
If left unglazed, body stains remain pale and subtle. In these samples, 2–10 per cent of body stain was added to a porcelain body and left unglazed.

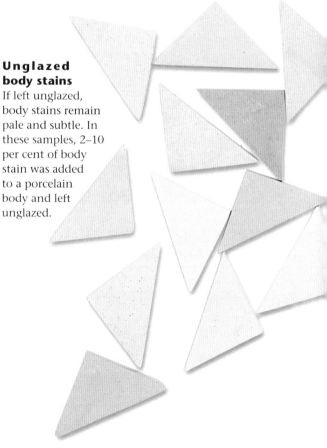

ON-GLAZE COLOURS Strictly speaking, most on-glaze decorating colours are enamels rather than glazes. They are designed for decorating glazed pots, generally by painting with a brush, followed by a low firing which is usually between 700°C and 800°C, depending on the brand, firing time and type of ware. Metallic and lustre colours fall into the on-glaze category.

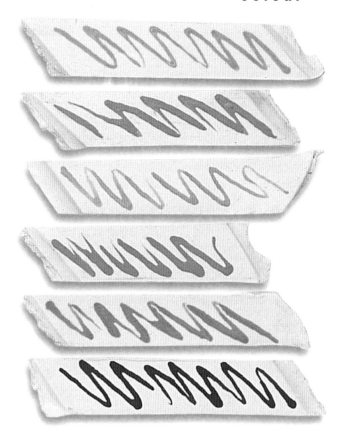

Potter's pens Underglaze colours in pen form, potter's pens have special nibs for easy drawing and writing on to biscuit-ware. Depending on the brand, the colours can be fired up to stoneware temperatures.

Underglaze colours for painting These can be used like powder paints and applied to biscuit-ware or unglazed pots with a brush. They should be mixed with a special medium.

COLOUR: DECORATING SLIPS

The first slips were simply clay body mixed with water and were painted or trailed on to the pot as decoration. These early slips were mainly red, black and white – the colours of natural clay. Sometimes they were burnished, sometimes covered with a basic lead glaze.

Today, the choice of colours is wider and the glazes safer, but the actual techniques of slip decoration have changed very little over several thousand years. Although the demonstrations shown here have a modern feel, they in fact represent some of the very earliest pottery decorating techniques.

MIXING SLIPS Coloured decorating slips can be bought pre-mixed and ready to use. If you prefer to make your own, make sure the slip has the same shrinkage rate as the clay to which it is applied. If not, the slip is liable to crack or shrink during or after firing. One way around the problem is to use the clay body to make the slip. If your clay is light or white, this is fine. If not, a red or dark clay body will affect any colouring stain and darken the colour of the slip.

An alternative solution is to mix a white slip from ball clay or from 60 per cent ball clay and 40 per cent china clay – a good general-purpose recipe – and add colouring stains and oxides as required.

Slip made from powder clay is best made by adding dry ingredients to water. If you are making slip from a plastic clay body, you will first need to break the clay into small pieces and cover these with water until the lumps have disintegrated.

APPLYING SLIP The thickness of the slip will depend on how it is to be used. For example, trailing and feathering are best done with a fairly thick slip that does not spread too much; for marbling, the slip colours should be more fluid.

As a general rule, decorating slips are used on stiff or leather-hard clay. To apply one colour over another, the first colour must be allowed to dry slightly until the slip loses its gloss. This process can be speeded up considerably by using a hairdryer.

LAYING FLAT COLOUR

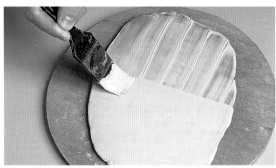

Using a very soft brush, start by applying a layer of colour in straight, parallel strokes. When this has dried slightly, apply a second coat, taking the strokes in the opposite direction. Continue building up the slip in this way until you have a good flat colour.

SGRAFITTO

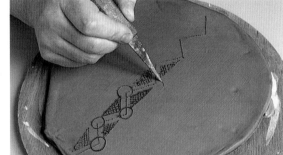

A sharp tool can be used to scratch pattern and texture into wet or leather-hard clay. Here, a special sgraffito tool is used on a coloured slip to reveal the clay underneath. Sgraffito can also be done with a knitting needle, scalpel or any sharp tool.

PRINTING

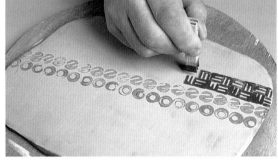

Coloured slips can be used for printed decoration made with a variety of tools. Here, repeat patterns are made using potter's printing sticks. These useful little tools are generally used for impressing patterns into the clay, but they work equally well for printing colour.

COMBING TEXTURE

Traditional combed patterns can be made in wet slip using a hair comb, fork or other suitable implement. For broad or irregular patterns, you can make your own decorating comb from stiff cardboard.

MARBLING

1 Start by pouring a few blobs of two or more colours on to a clay base. NOTE Slips for marbling should be slightly runnier than those used for other decorative slip techniques.

2 Swivel the clay briskly, first in one direction and then the other, until the colours begin to run and blend. If necessary, use a needle or other pointed tool to help drag the colours into each other.

FEATHERING

1 Start by trailing straight parallel lines across the leather-hard clay with coloured slip. If you are using two or more colours, apply one colour at a time, leaving enough space between the lines for subsequent colours to be added.

2 While the trailed colours are still wet, take the tip of a feather and drag this across the trailed lines. Drag in one direction first, leaving enough space between the dragged marks to go back and drag the colour in the opposite direction.

PAPER RESIST

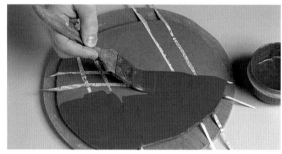

1 Cut or tear a design from newspaper or other absorbent paper and lay this on the surface of the leather-hard clay. Using a very soft brush, paint the decorating slip evenly over the surface.

2 If you are using more than one colour, lay further newspaper patterns on the slightly dried slip. Still using a soft brush, apply a second colour over the first coloured slip and the new patterns.

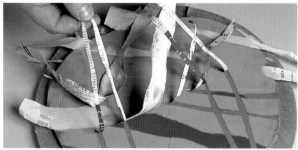

SLIP TRAILING

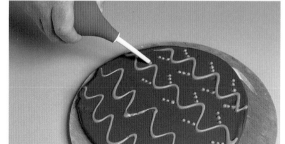

3 Finally, remove all the paper to reveal the layered design. The newspaper can become soggy under the layers of slip, and you may need a needle or scalpel blade to find and lift any paper that has become buried in the slip.

For trailing lines, fill the trailer with slip and draw the colour across the clay, squeezing gently. The slip trailer should be just touching the surface of the clay. For dots and smaller marks, squeeze out the slip, then lift the trailer clear of the wet colour.

MANGANESE AND COBALT OXIDE

Spongeware teapot made by the Wetheriggs Pottery, Cumbria, in 1917. This and similar teapots were made to order and often inscribed with the client's name. The striking decoration is done with manganese and cobalt oxides sponged over a white slip. It is then covered with a clear glaze before being fired in a coal-fired kiln.

COBALT OXIDE

A lidded bowl by Jonathan Snell, c1980. The earthenware pot is decorated with white slip and bold brush strokes of cobalt oxide. The pot and lid are then dipped in clear glaze and fired in a coal-fired kiln.

COPPER OXIDE

A serving platter by E.B. Fishleigh of the Fremmington pottery in Devon, c1900. The platter is decorated with copper before being dipped in a clear glaze. The incised decoration is made by scraping a bold wavy line through the raw glaze before firing.

WHITE SLIP

A slip-decorated salt kit, or salt 'pig', dating from 1890. A traditional 'waves and dots' design is trailed in white slip over an earthenware pot before being dipped in clear glaze. The kits were popular as presents, specially commissioned, and usually incorporating the date and the name of the owner or recipient in the design.

FUMED OXIDES AND SEAWEED

A contemporary pit-fired vessel by Jacqui Atkin. The burnished pot is smoke fired in a pit, surrounded by seaweed and various metallic oxides. The random pattern comes from colours released by the oxides and seaweed during firing.

FIRING: THE ELECTRIC KILN

A small electric kiln is easy to use and simple to install. Depending on its size, it is run from either a 13 amp socket or a 30 amp cooker-type connection. The latter should be installed by an electrician.

Firing controls differ depending on the type, make and size of kiln. However, once you are familiar with the firing control fitted to your particular kiln, it will need little skill to operate.

WHICH KILN? Choice of kiln depends very much on available space and the scale of work involved. For very small ceramics, such as pieces of jewellery, the smallest test kiln will probably be sufficient.

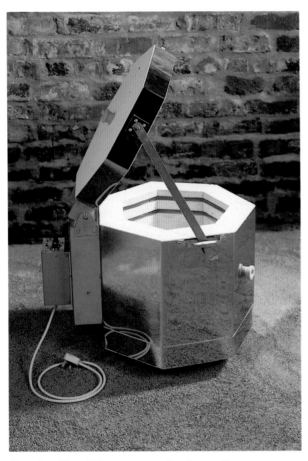

Top-loading kiln An example of a small top-loading electric kiln with an automatic firing controller. This model is small enough to be plugged into an ordinary 13 amp power socket. Larger models may need a cooker-type connection.

The main decision is whether to invest in a top-loading or front-loading kiln. A top-loading kiln is cheaper to buy and takes up less space in a small studio or spare room, because you do not have to allow space for the door to open. It is also lighter and can be pushed out of the way when not in use. Front-loading, or oven-type, kilns are more expensive to buy but are generally cheaper to maintain than top-loaders. They are stronger and more durable, but this also renders them heavier and therefore less portable.

On the whole, a front-loading kiln is easier to load because the kiln shelves can stay in the same position. The kiln is filled and emptied in much the same way as an electric oven. Conversely, when filling a top-loader there is a risk that specks of clay or glaze will fall unnoticed on to pots lower down and spoil the glaze firing.

There are pros and cons with both types, but in the end the choice depends on personal requirements. The main considerations are size, location and available space.

SAFETY AND VENTILATION The outside of a kiln can get very hot, especially if it is a top-loading type. If children or animals are likely to come into contact with a kiln, it is a good idea to fit a kiln cage or to erect a screen around the kiln. Electric cables should be kept well away from the sides or top of a hot kiln and extension leads avoided, because they may overheat and become a fire hazard. Correct fusing is important, and fuses must be of the appropriate rating.

The kiln should be installed in a well-ventilated space. This may be a room with cross-ventilation provided by two windows or similar openings, or the room should be fitted with an extractor fan in a window or outside wall. If neither of these is a possibility, the kiln itself should be fitted with an extraction system.

NOTE By law, a kiln must be fitted with a safety device which switches off the kiln when the door is opened.

KILN FURNITURE Kiln shelves, or batts, are made from a material which will withstand the highest firing temperatures. This is usually carborundum, silicon carbide or a high-alumina mixture such as cordierite or sillimanite. The shelves are spaced and supported by props, which are usually tubular and come in varying lengths. Other types of prop are castellated and have turret-like tops which interlock and fit together to form adjustable supports.

Three supports per batt are usually sufficient in a small kiln. However, at higher temperatures, and especially if the batt is carrying a heavy load of pots, it may be necessary to support it with a central prop. Kiln furniture should always be arranged so that the props rather than the batts bear most of the load.

Other useful items are kiln stilts. These normally have three sharply pointed arms and are used to support the pot during firing.

LOADING A KILN A biscuit firing is simpler to load than a glaze or 'glost' firing, because pots can touch each other in the kiln and one pot can be put inside another. Lidded pots can and should be fired with their lids on, to ensure equal shrinkage and a better fit. Pots can be fired upside down and on their sides if this means better use of space. In a glost firing, glazed surfaces must not touch, or they will stick together.

In all firings, the kiln should be as evenly and closely packed as possible, and there should be a space of at least 2.5cm (1in) between the pot and the side of the kiln. If possible, tall pots should not be placed close to the sides of the kiln, because they may incline towards the element due to greater shrinkage on that side.

A thin layer of kiln or batt wash will protect the batts and help prevent glazed pots sticking to the shelf during firing. Also, all pots must be completely dry before firing.

FIRING TEMPERATURES Biscuit firing transforms a pot from raw clay into hard ceramic. The actual transformation takes place at around 500°–600°C, but biscuit firings are normally taken higher than this. The final temperature depends on whether or not the pot is to be glazed, and to some extent on the maker's personal preference. Usually a biscuit firing is somewhere between 850°C and 1100°C, but it may be slightly lower or higher.

Glaze firing temperatures depend on the type of clay. Stoneware glazes are usually fired between 1220°C and 1300°C, earthenware between 1050°C and 1150°C.

KILN CONTROLS A kiln may be fitted with one of several devices to control the firing. These range from basic shut-off mechanisms to sophisticated digital controls. The latter can be pre-set to determine not only the length and temperature of a firing but also different speeds of temperature increase that take place during the course of the firing.

CONES Pyrometric cones made from carefully controlled ceramic materials are designed to melt and bend at certain temperatures. There are several types of cone on the market, all numbered according to their approximate bending temperature. Cones are placed in the kiln near the spyhole so that they can be observed during firing. The speed of firing also affects the reaction of the cone, making it an extremely accurate indicator of a completed firing.

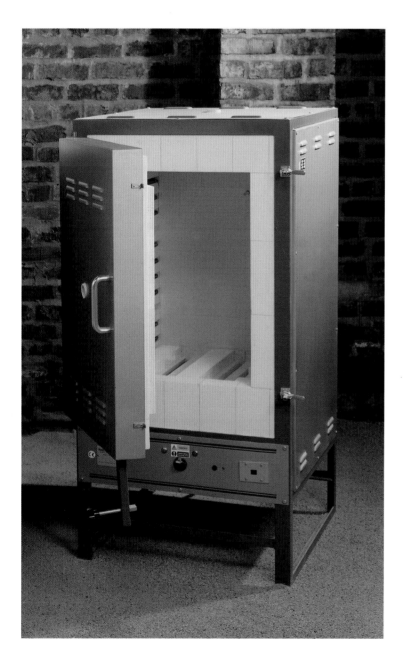

Front-loading kiln A front-loading kiln with a built-in firing control. Front-loading kilns are stacked and emptied in much the same way as an electric cooker.

SMOKE FIRING

Beautiful decorative patterns can be created by smoke firing a pot in sawdust or newspaper. However, as neither the temperature nor the consistency of these firings will be sufficient to fire the pot properly, it must first be biscuit fired in a normal kiln. Smoke firing is for decorating only.

The carbon patterns created by smoke firing are burned into the surface of the pot and are therefore permanent in normal conditions. However, if the pattern is not to your liking, it can be burned off completely by giving the pot another biscuit firing. You can then start again with the smoke firing, repeating this process if necessary until you get a result you like.

Because it is impossible to control the results of this type of firing completely, a typical smoked pattern is random and spontaneous – amorphous in shape, and ranging from black to pale grey in colour. Many potters like this surprise element, but others prefer to adapt the method in order to have more control over the finished decoration. The masking tape technique shown here is an example of this. Also, by adding oxides and other substances to the firing material it is possible to introduce a range of beautiful and subtle colours to vary the otherwise monochromatic patterns.

SMOKE FIRING IN SAWDUST The beauty of sawdust firing lies in its simplicity. Traditionally, this is done in a pit dug in the ground; today, sawdust firing is more commonly carried out in a metal dustbin. Small holes are sometimes punched around the bottom of the bin to produce a slight draught, which will help the sawdust to burn. An alternative is to push in one or two metal pipes, leaving their ends sticking out of the sawdust to provide some ventilation. Another type of sawdust kiln can be built from kiln bricks on a flat, solid surface.

For the firing, the pot is placed on a layer of sawdust in the kiln, then covered with more sawdust. This is ignited at the top and left to burn and smoulder until the sawdust has burned away and the kiln has cooled down.

A sawdust firing can take anything from a couple of hours to several days, depending on its size, ventilation, and the type of sawdust used. Fine sawdust is slow-burning and tends to create dense black marks; coarse sawdust burns faster but creates paler marks. Wood shavings or even small pieces of kindling wood will often burn away in an hour or two. Scrunched-up newspapers can be pushed in around the outside of the sawdust to help combustion.

SMOKE FIRING WITH NEWSPAPER Smoked patterns can often be achieved instantly by placing the pot in a few scrunched-up newspapers and setting fire to them. However, it is more usual to place the pot and newspapers in a metal bin, where the flames can be contained and the results monitored.

MASKING TAPE AND SLURRY Both the sawdust and newspaper firings shown here were done using masking tape and slurry – a thick slip made from clay and water. The masking tape is cut up to the desired design and stuck to a burnished, biscuit-fired pot. Other materials have been used successfully and it is worth experimenting to discover different effects. However, masking tape burns well and gives a particularly crisp result.

The taped pot is covered with two or three layers of thick slurry, or until the tape becomes invisible. The slurry is allowed to dry and the pot is fired in either newspaper or sawdust (sawdust usually creates a softer, less defined pattern than newspaper). The masking tape burns away underneath the slurry, leaving a carbonized black pattern.

PRECAUTIONS The sudden changes in temperature as the pot gets hot or cools down can cause cracking. This is because the clay body cannot accommodate the expansions and contractions caused by the rapid change of heat.

This risk of cracking is minimized by choosing a clay with a good resistance to thermal shock. A grogged or 'open' body is best, with T-material generally regarded as one of the safest clays, either on its own or mixed with another clay body. Jacqui Atkin, who made the smoke-firing projects for this book, uses an equal mixture of T-material and porcelain for all her smoke-fired work. The risk of cracking is reduced if the pot is warmed before being put in the kiln, and also allowed to cool down before being removed.

Some shapes are more resilient than others – small, enclosed forms being the safest, large bowls with thin rims the most vulnerable. The walls of the pot should be of even thickness; hand-built and slabbed vessels must be joined very securely at the edges.

A word of warning: this type of firing inevitably creates a lot of smoke, so try to find a spot where you will not annoy the neighbours.

NOTE The Coiled Bottle on page 120 is smoke fired with newspaper, and the Smoke-fired Jug on page 114 is smoked in sawdust.

NEWSPAPER FIRING

1 The pot is placed in a bin of lightly crumpled newspapers (some potters find it useful to make a few small holes near the bottom of the bin to help combustion).

2 More crumpled newspaper is placed over the pot, making sure it is packed evenly but without making it too compact.

3 The newspaper is ignited in more than one place.

4 The bin is covered with a piece of chicken wire to prevent pieces of burning paper flying out, and left until the newspaper has burned away.

5 When the kiln has cooled down, the pot is examined. If the slurry is black, the pot is ready to be removed and cleaned (it does not matter if some slurry drops off as the pot is lifted). If the slurry is pale or patchy, more newspaper is added and the pot given a second firing.

SAWDUST FIRING

1 The pot is placed in the kiln on top of a layer of wood shavings. The sawdust kiln used here is a metal bin punctured with small holes.

2 The pot is covered with sawdust and a few newspapers are pushed in around the outside edge of the sawdust to help ignition and get the fire under way.

3 The newspapers are ignited in several places to encourage the flames to burn evenly in the kiln.

4 When the flames are going, the lid is placed to cover the bin partially. The chicken wire creates a ventilation gap between the lid and the bin. The kiln remains like this until the sawdust has burned away and the kiln cooled down. The smoked pot can then be lifted out and cleaned.

RAKU FIRING

Raku originated from Japan, where its name means 'happiness' or 'enjoyment'. The firing technique, which is something between a conventional glazing and a sawdust firing, has been traced back to the sixteenth century and possibly earlier. However, the combination of stunning colours and a rapid firing cycle have made raku one of the most popular of all contemporary ceramic techniques.

A typical raku pot is first biscuit fired, then glazed and fired quickly to a low temperature in a special raku kiln. Most modern raku firings are between 800°C and 1000°C, although Japanese potters sometimes fired their pots to a far higher temperature. After firing, the pot is removed from the kiln while still hot. Depending on the effect required, it is then usually reduced and carbonized in sawdust, wood shavings, leaves or other combustible material. More reduction can be achieved by placing a metal tin or drum over the pot and combustible material, to halt further oxidization and prevent the smoke escaping. Alternatively, use a metal bin or pot with a lid.

Some potters plunge the still-hot pot into cold water or spray it with water after an initial reduction, in order to fix the colours and patterns. However, this can be risky and must be done with care. Pots are easily lost during this process due to the sudden change in temperature.

Those parts of the pot which have not been glazed will burn to a dramatic black during the carbonizing and reduction processes.

RAKU GLAZES A raku glaze is high in flux and has a low melting point. Typical raku fluxes are low-temperature lead and alkaline frits. In most raku glazes the flux content is 80–95 per cent, the rest being mainly alumina, or clay body.

Oxides are frequently used in raku decoration, either mixed with the glaze or applied in the form of slip and painted stain. The results are unpredictable but can be stunning. Copper is the most effective colouring oxide, and is capable of producing a whole spectrum of vivid colours, depending on the glaze, the reduction process and the clay body.

Crackle glazes are particularly associated with raku pots. This is partly because many low-firing glazes craze or crackle naturally when cooled rapidly, as in the raku process. The decorative possibilities of this effect have been explored and developed by many raku artists.

CLAY BODIES As with sawdust firing, any clay which can survive the speedy firing and cooling process is suitable for use with raku. Special raku clays are formulated for the purpose. However, depending on the size and construction of the pots, any grogged or open body will generally be fine. T-material is probably the best choice, either on its own or mixed with another clay.

SLIP RESIST Contemporary potters have created and developed their own versions of the raku process. One such technique involves coating the burnished biscuit-fired pot with a thick clay slurry and then covering this with any type of glaze – not necessarily a raku glaze. The pot is then fired and carbonized as described above.

When the pot has cooled, the baked slurry and glaze are removed to reveal the carbonized patterns which have formed on the surface of the pot. These vary from a delicate lace pattern to mottled or marbled effects. Oxides and even sugar can be added to the slip to produce their own characteristic effects.

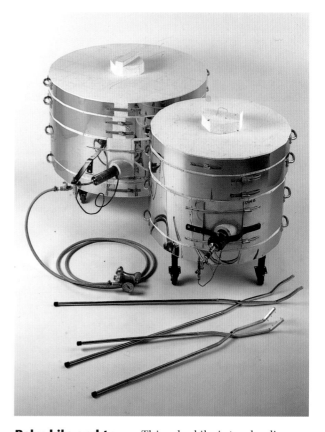

Raku kiln and tongs This raku kiln is top-loading, fuelled with propane gas, and comes with a burner, heat regulator and kiln stand. The tongs are specially made for pulling hot raku pots from the kiln.

1 The biscuit-fired ware is placed in the kiln, making sure no glazed areas are touching. Here, the unglazed edge of the lid is propped on the unglazed rim of the casket, so that the lid can be lifted easily with the tongs. The pot is warmed slightly before being placed in the kiln, to avoid a sudden change of temperature which might cause damage.

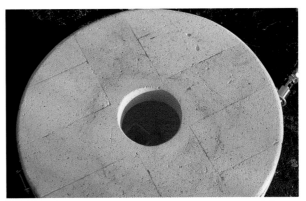

2 The propane burner is lit and the strength of flame increased gradually to avoid thermal shock. The pot, which can be seen here through the ventilation hole in the top of the kiln, is ready when the glaze becomes shiny and fluid-looking. The firing time depends on the kiln and rate of firing, but in a small kiln a firing can take about 20 minutes, longer if the kiln is being fired from cold.

3 The kiln lid is quickly removed and, using heatproof gloves and raku tongs, the pieces are taken quickly from the kiln and placed in a metal bin on a layer of sawdust. The red-hot pot ignites the sawdust.

4 A tightly fitting metal lid is placed on the bin and the pots left until they are cool.

5 The lid is removed to reveal the fired pots, which can be washed and gently scrubbed to remove the burned sawdust and bring out the colours.

6 If the carbon is stubborn, clean carefully with a toothbrush and a little soap. Shiny glazes can be brought up by buffing with a rag. Dry copper raku glazes are not waterproof and should not be washed.

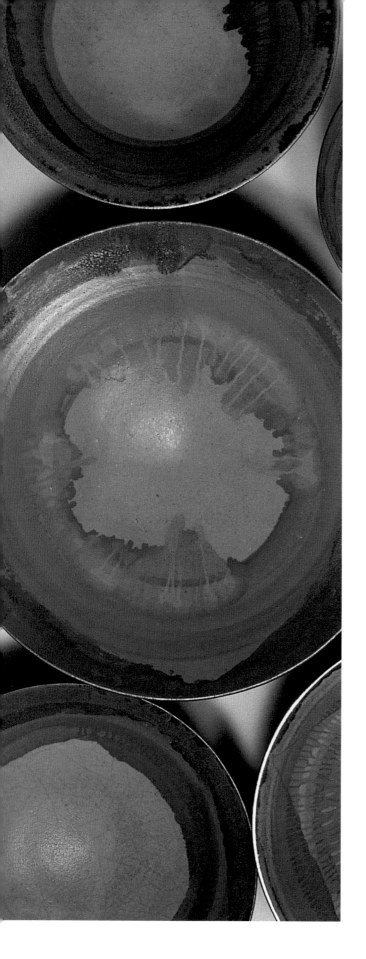

the projects

The 20 projects featured in the following pages provide a fascinating and detailed insight into how each artist works. The demonstrations show clearly how the materials are used, and how the pieces are constructed and decorated. Hopefully, they will provide inspiration, and encourage you to have a go yourself. However, it is important to remember that each project represents a personal approach, an individual way of working.

It is a mistake to attempt to reproduce exactly the work of another artist, and in any case will inevitably lead to disappointment. Ceramics is not a precise art. No two glaze mixtures are the same, and no two firings produce the same results. Also, in the long run it is more fun and more constructive to develop your own ideas.

For example, the materials listed with each project were those used by the potter. It is not suggested that these are the only materials; in fact, they could and should be used as a starting point. For example, colour is a matter of personal choice, so try to develop your own glazes and slips rather than copying someone else's.

Please note that the materials listed with each project are the ceramic materials – the clay, glaze, colouring oxides and so on – and materials directly involved with the ceramic process. Tools and general materials such as masking tape are not listed.

DECORATING AND MAKING TECHNIQUES

Certain techniques used in the projects are also of general interest or could be used in an altogether different context. For example, the slipping and joining technique used in the Raku Casket on page 60 is a standard method

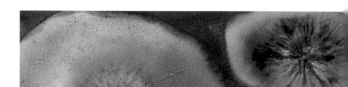

for joining clay on many types of hand-built pots, not just on raku caskets.

In these cases, the technique in question is featured separately for easy reference under the heading Making Technique or Decorating Technique.

THE OUTDOOR PROJECTS

It is impossible to describe the excitement of an outdoor firing – you have to be there to appreciate it. No photograph can capture exactly the thrill of seeing the liquid-looking glazed pots being pulled red-hot from a raku kiln, or a smoke-fired pot revealed black and encrusted in the bottom of the bin after the fire has finally died down.

Three of the projects in this section – the Smoke-fired Jug, Coiled Bottle and Raku Casket – are fired in the open air. In order to understand fully the making process of these pieces you should also refer to pages 36–37 and 38–39, where the techniques of raku and smoke firing are covered in more detail.

There are many variable factors with outside firing. A cold wind affects the kiln temperature and firing time, and a wet or damp atmosphere can adversely affect a raku glaze, which in any case is unpredictable. Smoke-fired markings are not always attractive after the first firing: the pattern may be too pale or uneven, and you may well want to give it another go or start again from scratch.

Inevitably, there will be the occasional disaster, such as pots cracking. To avoid disappointment, it is a good idea to allow for this and make a few similar pieces to be fired in the same session.

seated dog

Geoff Fuller has kept dogs for 30 years and knows exactly how they move, stand, lie and sit. Even so, he describes his models as 'fairly impromptu'. Some of his clay dogs are realistic, others more experimental, but in all his models the features, form and pose of the animals are very slightly exaggerated. This is done deliberately to make the creatures look alive – a trick which he admits could easily be overdone by an inexperienced artist.

The clay dogs are not necessarily made to look like a particular breed, but will often contain essential expressions and poses of several different breeds. For example, the dog modelled in this project is described as 'whippet-like' rather than pure whippet.

Each part of the animal's body is made separately. The pieces are then assembled carefully to ensure they do not come apart during firing. The figures are dipped in slip and glazed, so there is no biscuit firing.

MATERIALS

Red earthenware clay and slip

White decorating slip

Copper oxide

Cobalt oxide

Lead basilicate glaze: 80% lead basilicate,
    20% white earthenware, plus 2% flint,
    3% bentonite, 2–3% iron oxide

one The base is made from clay rolled to about 1cm (⅓in) thick and cut with a slightly bevelled edge using a potter's knife. This is smoothed and evened by pressing all round with a small wooden board. While the base is left to dry slightly, the body of the dog is made from a tapering sausage shape, rolled from a piece of clay with more pressure being exerted at the tapered end.

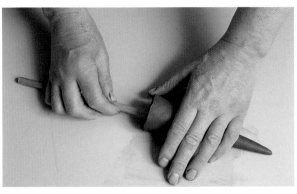

two The tapered body is hollowed by pushing a stick down the centre of the sausage from the thickest end and then pressing down on the stick as rolling continues. The hollowing is necessary in order to achieve a flexible form.

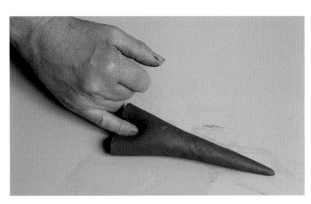

three The body forming begins by pressing down on the broad end of the hollow cone to flatten it a little. The flattened area forms the dog's haunches.

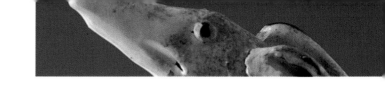

four Gradually the form is squeezed and modelled to suggest the position of the waist and chest. More squeezing and pulling produces an elongated, slightly exaggerated whippet's body.

five When a satisfactory form has been achieved, the haunches of the dog are dipped in slip and joined to the base by pressing with the edge of a small board.

six Two small sausages are rolled for the back legs. The haunches and lower part of the body are modelled and manipulated to form a more naturalistic shape.

seven The pointed shape of the head is emphasized and this is set at a deliberately exaggerated angle. Long, tapering shapes are rolled for the front legs. Each leg is fixed in position and pressed firmly on to the base. The front legs are slightly bent at this stage to allow for shrinkage.

eight   The tail is a long, thin roll of clay. This is dipped in slip and fixed by pressing.

nine   The whippet's nose is pulled to an even longer point and tweaked into a more upright position. The ears are small pieces of clay, flattened and then lightly rolled. These, too, are dipped in slip and fixed by pressing and smoothing.

ten   A piece of wood is used to impress the mouth, which is slightly smiling to give a sense of facial expression.

eleven   Tiny balls of clay form the slightly protruding eyes. These are made a few hours in advance and allowed to dry until slightly firm. This prevents them from getting flattened as they are attached. To model the feet, the dog is placed on the edge of the board and the toes impressed with the edge of a piece of wood.

twelve

The statue is allowed to dry until leather hard, before being dipped in white slip made from ball clay and water mixed to the consistency of double cream. The correct hardness of the model is crucial – it must be dry enough to absorb the water from the slip, but not so dry that it disintegrates with the moisture.

thirteen

The white dog is decorated with coloured slip applied with a brush, sponge or slip trailer. Finally, the model is allowed to dry before being dipped in a lead basilicate glaze and fired to 1040°–1060°C.

DECORATING TECHNIQUE

Using coloured slips

Coloured slips are best applied with a soft oriental brush and even then the technique calls for a little practice.

The most effective approach is to load the brush well and then to dribble the colour from the tip of the bristles on to the decorated surface.

For a powdery or speckled appearance, try applying coloured slips with a sponge, dabbing lightly to allow the underlying colour to show through. This blue slip is made by adding cobalt oxide to white slip.

Slip can also be applied with a slip trailer to give a good thick coat of colour.

porcelain plaque

Paul Scott is well known for his painted porcelain, especially his plaques and wall murals. The latter are made up of numerous interlocking shapes, similar to the three used in this project.

Paul describes painting on porcelain as being similar to working with watercolour paints. The pure white of the porcelain clay represents the paper, and the powdered underglaze colours are the paints. As with watercolours, ceramic pigments are first mixed on a palette and then applied with a soft brush.

However, although white porcelain looks like watercolour paper it is far more absorbent. Colours soak quickly into the porous surface and the brush must be very well loaded with colour in order to get a continuous, flowing line.

The first stages of this painting are simply blocks of colour – broad brush strokes of paint which are carefully placed in relation to the shapes of the three biscuit-fired pieces. This almost abstract arrangement of colours is then developed and transformed into a recognizable landscape with fields, hills, trees and buildings.

Unlike ceramic glazes, most of these commercially prepared pigments do not change colour when they are fired. In other words, the colours on the palette are more or less the same as those on the finished piece as it is taken from the kiln. Notable exceptions include cobalt blue and high-temperature red. The former is a deep, intense blue which is pale mauve in powder form; the latter fires to bright red but is pale pink before firing.

MATERIALS

Porcelain clay

Underglaze colours: cobalt blue, lime green, yellow, egg yellow, Persian green, apple green, high-temperature red, black, grey, cadmium red

Potclays semi-porcelain transparent glaze

MAKING TECHNIQUE

Using a harp

For plaques and other slabwork, clay can be cut quickly and evenly with a potter's harp. For making large slabs, remove the plastic covering from a bag of clay and slice through the whole block. If necessary, the slabs can then be rolled to the required thickness.

Set the wire in the appropriate notch to cut the clay to the thickness you want using a single continuous stroke.

Remove each slab as it is cut and keep the slabs moist by wrapping in plastic until you are ready to use them.

DECORATING TECHNIQUE

Mixing colour

Ceramic pigments are similar to powder paints and can be mixed on a palette to produce a wide range of colours and tones.

If you are working on a white background, mix the colours on a white plate or saucer – this way, you can see the colours as they will appear in the painting. Add small amounts of water and underglaze medium to the powdered colours as required and apply them with a soft brush.

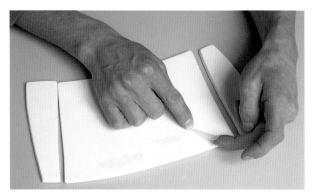

one The design for the plaque is based on a black-and-white ink drawing, in which all the main areas of the landscape are depicted as graphic shapes of pattern and texture. The three-piece plaque is cut from a slab of porcelain and biscuit fired to 1000°C. Before starting to paint, the clouds and chimney smoke are cut from masking tape and pressed into position on the sky area.

two Using a soft hake brush, cobalt blue is painted across the masked sky area in broad horizontal strokes. The strokes are graded, getting paler towards the horizon – an effect achieved by dipping one side of the brush deeper in the colour than the other. The masking tape is removed and the painted sky given a light spray of water to give the clouds and the horizon a soft, slightly mottled texture.

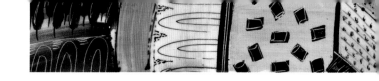

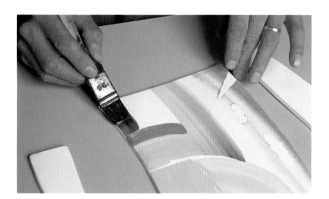

three A rounded hill in the foreground is suggested with a broad curve of lime green mixed with yellow. Sunny fields and distant fields are painted in mixtures of yellow, egg yellow, Persian green, apple green and lime green, with a bold stripe of high-temperature red in the foreground.

four Round red shapes are painted on a bright yellow field with a rigger brush – this will eventually be an orchard of fruit trees. The landscape is built up as a series of patterns: stubby black marks made with a flat brush for the bales of straw, and Persian green with a Chinese brush for the cypress trees. Other colours – the reds, greens and yellows – are strengthened by overpainting.

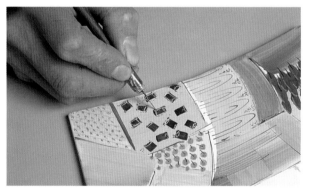

five Distant buildings are painted in grey. Fine lines, drawn with the tip of a rigger brush, look similar to pen and ink, and these are used to define the coloured fields. Details, such as the tufts of grass and foliage, are also added with the rigger tip. Using a sharp craft knife, fine lines are scratched into the painted colour to create highlights on the bales and trees, and furrows in the fields. These linear details are taken from the drawing.

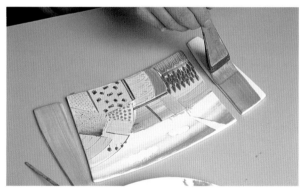

six One of the fields is spattered with colour to give the impression of flowers, while the rest of the picture is masked with pieces of paper. Bold black lines, applied with a brush, are used to define some of the larger areas. The curtain sections are painted in cadmium red with fine yellow and cobalt-blue stripes. Finally, the pieces are glazed with semi-porcelain transparent glaze and fired to 1200°C.

porcelain earrings

'Rather like making the stones under one's feet' is how Sarah Perry describes her work. She says she is a potter because she enjoys the basic feel of clay – its versatility and the actual making process. She also likes the idea that a work can be stopped at any point and made permanent by firing.

Although best known for thrown stoneware vessels decorated with brilliant colours and rich lustres, Sarah also enjoys making porcelain jewellery. Her earrings and brooches started as kiln fillers, but have now become an important part of her work. She prefers simple shapes because of their timeless quality – some of her designs have been going for several years without becoming dated.

Striking colours are enhanced by proprietary lustre glazes which may be gold, silver or bronze. Sarah's own jewellery colours tend to vary from pale duck-egg green to brilliant blues, depending on the stain or oxide she uses in the matt porcelain glaze. However, she recommends that anyone interested in making jewellery should try out some of the many bright colours now available in the high-firing range of stains.

Because lustre glazes take on the finish of the glaze to which they are applied, the gold lustres on the earrings have a fairly matt finish, similar to the matt glaze underneath.

MATERIALS

Porcelain clay

Matt porcelain glaze plus colouring stains

Metallic lustre glaze

Earring clips

one The porcelain clay is rolled out very thinly on a sheet of silicate; the porous surface absorbs moisture from the clay, making it stiff enough to cut and work on almost immediately. For the circular earrings, round shapes are cut from the clay using a small pastry cutter. A sharp food-chopping blade provides a clean edge when cutting out triangles and other geometric shapes.

two The edges of the shapes are neatened and softened by wiping with a piece of damp sponge, before being biscuit fired to a temperature of 960°C.

three The biscuit-fired earring shapes are dipped in matt porcelain glaze plus the chosen stain and laid reverse side down on newspaper.

four   Glaze is removed from the reverse side of the shapes using a straight-edged metal kidney or fettling tool.

five   A damp sponge is used to remove the residue of glaze to ensure that the shapes do not stick to the kiln shelves. They are then fired to a temperature of 1280°C.

six   A metallic lustre band is painted around the edges of each piece. The straight-edged shapes are painted freehand, while a whirler is used for round shapes. The earrings are fired once more to 800°C.

seven   Finally, a clip is stuck to the reverse side of each earring with epoxy resin glue applied with a matchstick.

torn
lustre brooch

Lustre glazes reflect the type of surface they are applied to. Over a matt glaze they become matt; over a gloss glaze they are shiny and reflective. On a biscuit surface, they tend to lose their lustrous qualities altogether and can appear simply as rather dull colours.

The lustre glaze range includes many iridescent colours and mother-of-pearl effects, as well as metallic finishes such as gold, silver, platinum, bronze and copper. Sarah Perry has experimented with many lustre glazes, and for the metallic finishes on her reflective brooches she recommends first glazing the biscuit-fired brooches with black or any dark, high-firing, glossy glaze. The lustres are then applied over the fired gloss glaze to produce a highly reflective metallic finish.

Essentially, then, for a reflective lustre effect the piece must be fired three times: a biscuit firing, a glossy underglaze firing, and a lustre firing. The final lustre firing is a low one – depending on the manufacturer's instructions, the firing temperature for lustre glazes is usually 800°C or below.

Lustres are far more expensive than other glazes – ideal for jewellery and decorative details, but costly to use on a large scale. However, a little goes a long way. The glazes should be applied thinly, and are diluted with special lustre thinner. It is important to keep a separate brush for each lustre glaze as the colours contaminate easily. Also, lustres give off fumes during firing, so it essential to have a properly ventilated kiln space and to follow the safety regulations.

MATERIALS

Porcelain clay

Dark gloss glaze suitable for porcelain

Metallic lustre glaze

Brooch pin

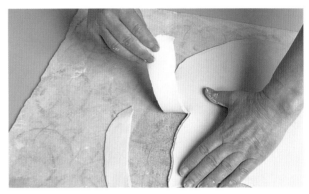

one Strips of porcelain clay are torn randomly from a sheet of thinly rolled porcelain. An attractive torn edge is created by holding the slab on the board with one hand and tearing upwards with the other.

two The torn strips are arranged in pairs (usually a brooch is made of two strips), care being taken to match pieces which look good together.

three The edges are overlapped slightly, and the area to be joined is scored with a knife and moistened with water.

torn lustre brooch

four The pieces are laid in position, care being taken not to spoil the crispness of the torn edges by overhandling.

five The overlapped edges are lightly pressed together and smoothed with a finger to ensure a firm join.

six The brooch is biscuit fired to a temperature of 980°C. It is then glazed with a dark-coloured, glossy, high-temperature glaze and fired to the recommended temperature. Here the brooch is being covered with lustre glaze, ready for its final firing at 800°C.

seven The back of the brooch is left unglazed, all accidental splashes having been wiped off the reverse side before firing. Finally, the pin is stuck to the reverse side of the brooch, using epoxy resin applied with a matchstick to the unglazed clay.

raku casket

Blown vinyl wallpaper is used to make the unusual decorative texture on this raku casket. The wallpaper can be bought from most DIY or decorating stores and is available in a surprising variety of swirling, abstract textures. This design is imprinted from one of the coarser designs. An alternative is anaglypta wallpaper, which has more formal designs and often incorporates flowers, leaves and geometric shapes.

This typically slab-built pot is constructed from leather-hard or stiff clay, cut with sharp, clean lines. The slabs may be cut vertically and joined at right angles, or cut at an angle of 45 degrees and joined by mitring, as in this project.

Jacqui Atkin, who designed and made the casket, uses silica board for rolling clay slabs. This is a time-saving method, because the silica absorbs the moisture from the clay, which soon becomes stiff enough to form into workable slabs.

Because the patterned surface of the vinyl wallpaper comes off on the damp clay, each card template can only be used once. However, for a longer-lasting template, the card and vinyl can be coated with a weak solution of PVA adhesive.

A raku crackle glaze is used here, but you can use any finish you like to complete the casket.

MATERIALS

Card for templates
Blown vinyl wallpaper
PVA adhesive
Clay: 50% T-material, 50% porcelain
Raku crackle glaze

one Templates are cut from porous card for the base and sides of the casket and the top and sides of the lid. The position of the decorative panels is marked on the templates for the lid top and the sides of the casket. Pieces of blown vinyl wallpaper are cut to the size of each panel and stuck in place with PVA adhesive.

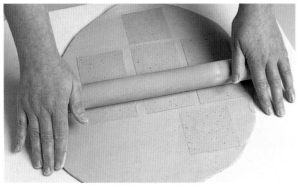

two The templates are placed vinyl side down on a sheet of rolled clay and rolled firmly and evenly with a rolling pin. The clay is then left to dry until it is stiff or leather hard.

three The clay slabs are cut out with a sharp craft knife and ruler, using the card edges as a guide.

MAKING TECHNIQUE

Scoring and joining

To ensure that a constructed pot does not come apart during drying or glazing, it is important to join the sections carefully. The edges of the stiff or leather-hard clay must be roughened, either by scoring with a knife or using a stiff brush. The roughened edges are then moistened by using a stiff brush or toothbrush and working in enough water to create a slip on the edges. Alternatively, you can mix and apply slip separately.

The locating rim on this casket is an important feature. Not only does it hold the lid securely in place, but it also acts as a strengthening strip for the sides of the casket, which otherwise tend to warp inwards during firing.

Make sure the edge of the clay is well roughened and thoroughly moistened with water or slip made from the same clay body.

For added strength, make a small coil and push this into the joint.

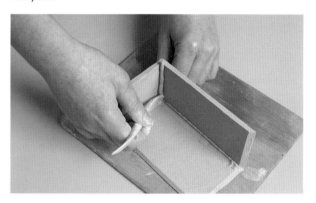

Use a wooden modelling tool to blend the coil smoothly into the constructed pot.

four When the card templates are lifted from each slab, the top surface of the vinyl is left imprinted in the clay.

five The remains of the vinyl paper must be removed carefully, first by peeling off the larger pieces, then by picking off the smaller pieces using a needle. A few remaining flecks of paper are fine, and will be burned off in the kiln.

six The edges to be joined are mitred at an angle of 45 degrees. This is done using a craft knife and a ruler which itself has a mitred edge.

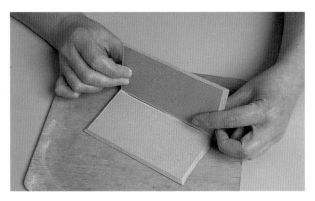

seven The mitred edges of the casket and lid are then scored, wet and stuck firmly together before being reinforced with a small coil.

eight The locating rim – the inside ridge which holds the lid in place – is cut from strips of stiff or leather-hard clay stuck in position on the inside of the casket.

nine The handles of the casket are made from tiny rolls of clay, cut to size and bent to form a slight curve. Each end of the handle is pressed lightly to flatten it and then fixed to the casket by stamping with a small wooden printing stick.

ten The dried casket is biscuit fired to 950°C. The edges around the textured panels are then painted with raku crackle glaze, taking care not to get any glaze on the inside edges or the locating rim, as this would cause the lid to stick during glazing.

eleven The casket is then fired in a raku kiln (see Raku firing on pages 38–39). After firing, it is cleaned well using warm water to reveal the glazed surface.

slip-decorated dish

The pretty pattern on this decorative dish is scratched into the surface of the clay to reveal the layers of coloured slip underneath. Unlike glazed pottery, the decoration on this dish is built into the clay instead of sitting on the surface – a quality which the potter, Jacqui Atkin, likes in her work.

Incised pattern, cut through a layer of clay to expose the contrasting colours underneath, is sometimes called 'sgraffito'. This is an ancient technique, which was used in many countries including China, Byzantia and the Middle East, where examples of sgraffitti-decorated pots date back more than a thousand years.

For the contemporary potter, specially made sgraffiti tools come in a variety of shapes to create different lines and effects. However, most clay-modelling tools work well, and excellent tools can be improvised from wire, metal and wood.

When handling the dish a lot during burnishing, a cotton glove will prevent finger marks appearing in the clay.

Because it is not glazed, the dish is mainly decorative. It is not waterproof and cannot be used for food.

MATERIALS

Clay: 50% T-material, 50% porcelain

Commercial coloured slips: blue, black and pink

White slip made from clay body

one The leather-hard dish is lifted from the mould and the edges tidied and levelled with a surformer. The edge should be tilted at a slight angle to prevent it acquiring a 'chopped off' look. A metal kidney is used to smooth and round off the sharp angles of the edge.

two A layer of blue slip is applied using a soft, flat brush. Smooth criss-cross strokes ensure a smooth, even finish. Further layers of coloured slip – blue, black, pink and white – are then applied to the top and underside of the leather-hard bowl, finishing with the white slip on top. Two or three coats of each colour ensure an effective result, each layer of slip being allowed to dry slightly before applying further layers.

three A polished stone is used to burnish the surface lightly (see Decorating technique on page 75). When burnishing the underside, the dish is propped on a wad of soft padding to prevent damaging the inside surface.

four For the sgrafitti decoration, a leaf-shaped template is cut from thin card. The position of each pattern on the rim is marked with a sharp metal tool. The same tool is used to trace around the leaf-shaped template – one in the centre of the base, and one on each side of this.

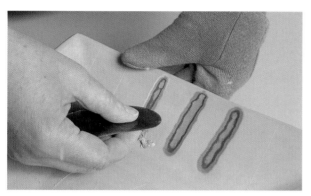

five Using the rounded end of a metal kidney, the layers of slip are scraped back to reveal the colours underneath. This is a slow, careful process, with one layer of colour being revealed at a time. As each pattern is completed, the surrounding area is burnished lightly before moving on to the next pattern.

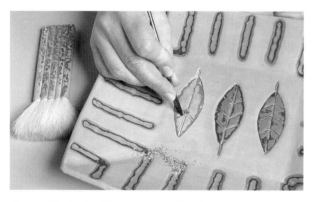

six The leaf pattern is scraped back in a similar way to reveal the pink, blue and black slips. If necessary, the flakes of clay can be brushed away with a soft brush. Finally, the dried dish is fired to a temperature of 950°C.

DECORATING TECHNIQUE

Painting coloured slips

Coloured decorating slips are usually applied to clay at the stiff or leather-hard stage. If the clay is too dry and absorbent, it will collapse. If several layers of slip are to be applied, each layer should be allowed to dry before you apply the next. A hairdryer is useful for speeding up this process.

Apply slip using a soft brush and light, even strokes. Unfired clay is fragile, so work carefully and support the vessel with your other hand as you paint.

MAKING TECHNIQUE

Using a press mould

A shallow press mould, made from fired clay or plaster of Paris, is one of the simplest ways of creating dishes and other clay forms. The clay is simply rolled, pressed into the mould, and left until it is stiff enough to take out. If your mould is made from plaster, it is important not to get flakes into the clay, because these will cause the work to split or bloat during firing. For this reason, you should avoid using metal tools near the press mould because these will scratch the plaster – use wooden tools instead.

Roll the clay to the thickness and size required. Lift this carefully and lower it into the mould, stretching the clay as little as possible. Smooth it down with a damp sponge.

When the dish has stiffened a little, cut away surplus clay from the rim using a wooden tool held horizontally. The clay can either be cut along the top of the mould, or cut lower down for a shallower dish. Leave the dish in the mould until it has shrunk away from the sides and is firm enough to handle.

fantastical fruits

Each of these exotic fantasy fruits starts as two pinch pots – small pots made by squeezing the clay between fingers and thumb. The pots are then joined together at the rims to form what their creator, Jacqui Atkin, describes as 'dinosaur eggs'. Although each piece is a product of her imagination and not intended to represent any particular fruit, all the objects are loosely based on a number of different natural forms, including fruits and vegetables.

Once the pinch pots have been joined, air is trapped in the resulting egg, making it impossible to alter the shape. It is therefore necessary to make a small hole in the egg before it can be modelled and squeezed into a fruit-like form.

At this stage, air can be squeezed gently out of the fruit. However, if too much air is squeezed out the fruit can collapse, so as soon as the modelling is complete the hole should be stopped up to preserve the shape.

The finished fruits can be glazed, smoked, or decorated with coloured slips like the one in the demonstration.

MATERIALS

Clay: 50% T-material, 50% porcelain

Slip made from clay body

Commercial green and yellow stains for colouring slip

one Each fruit is made from two pinch pots of the same size. These are allowed to stiffen a little – sufficient to retain their shape when joined together.

two The edges of the pots are scored and moistened with a toothbrush before being pushed firmly together.

three To strengthen the join, a small coil is pushed into the seam and blended in with a modelling tool (see Making technique on page 63).

four A wooden clay patter is used to pat the fruit into shape. This process also compacts the clay and helps to make the join more secure.

five A small hole is made in the rounded clay form, which is then squeezed and modelled to get the basic fruit shape. The fruit is held carefully and the air gently squeezed out as the fruit is pulled into shape and ridges are formed with the thumb.

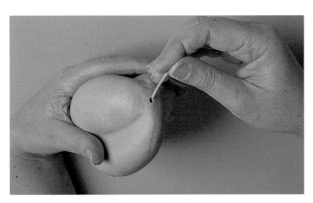

six When the basic modelling is complete, the hole is blocked up with a little clay. This keeps the air inside and prevents the form collapsing. A metal kidney is used to refine the shape of the fruit and smooth out the surface.

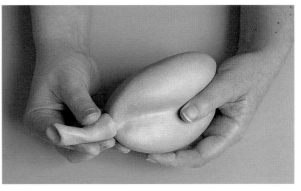

seven The stalk is made from a piece of clay pulled and pinched into shape. A small twist gives the stalk an organic feel. One end is left as a broad blob which is scored, moistened and pushed firmly on to the fruit, making sure no air is trapped in the join. Ridges and details on the stem are made with a wooden modelling tool.

MAKING TECHNIQUE

Making pinch pots

Pinch, or thumb, pots are made by pressing your thumb into a ball of clay and then pinching and squeezing the clay to form the walls of the pot.

Roll a piece of clay into a round ball and make a hole in the centre with your thumb, supporting the base with your other hand. Leave a base thickness of about 1cm (½in).

Keeping your thumb crooked to ensure the hole stays as small as possible early on, hold the pot between your thumb on the inside and your fingers on the outside. Pinch and thin the sides, revolving the pot slowly. Work round and round, smoothing and pinching at the same time.

As the wall of the pot gets gradually thinner, pinch the rim to keep it neat and even.

eight To colour the model, the stalk is painted with green slip and two layers of yellow slip are painted on to the surface of the fruit (see Decorating technique on page 69). When the yellow slip is dry, strips of torn wet newspaper are laid lengthways on the fruit.

nine The fruit is painted with green slip. The yellow slip is then dabbed on with a small sponge to create a speckled texture over the green.

DECORATING TECHNIQUE

Burnishing

Pots can be polished, or burnished, to give the surface a glossy shine. Burnishing is generally done at the leather-hard stage and is an alternative to glazing. However, a burnished pot is not usually watertight and is suitable only for holding dry goods and for decoration.

Burnishing should be done with an even pressure, usually in small, circular movements. Alternatively, larger objects can be burnished using long, even strokes to create a particularly smooth finish. Fingermarks show up on a burnished pot before it is fired, so it is a good idea to hold the work in a gloved hand during the burnishing process.

ten The newspaper is removed using a needle or other pointed tool to lift the end of each strip, which can then be pulled off.

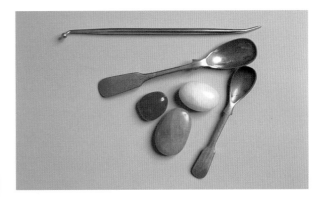

Any suitably shaped smooth object can be used as a burnishing tool – preferably one with a slightly convex surface. Possibilities include specially made metal and glass burnishers, pebbles, and plastic or metal teaspoons.

eleven When the clay and slip are leather hard, the fruit is burnished to create a glossy finish and fired to 950°C. It is important to make a small hole in the pot before firing, otherwise the trapped air will expand and cause the fruit to explode in the kiln.

landscape vase

Syl Macro's press-moulded vessels reflect her love of the countryside and the landscape around her home. Her designs are taken from photographs and sketches, and she has an eye for detail – for the patterns and textures which are built into her pots.

Each landscape vessel starts as a flat pattern – pieces of textured clay fitted together to form a patchwork of hills, fields and trees. The vase is formed by pressing the completed landscape into a plaster mould, a process which is carried out with great care in order to preserve the textures and surface patterns on the clay.

For this vase, paper pulp is mixed with the wet clay in order to strengthen it, both during the leather-hard stage and as it dries out prior to firing. This extra strength makes handling the vase easier, especially when it is being lifted from the mould, as at this point the fragile clay walls could easily collapse.

The textures in this landscape come from a number of unlikely sources, including lace, various embossed fabrics – even a string vest! However, almost any textured object or material – readily available examples include corrugated cardboard, wickerwork and hessian – can be rolled into a slab of wet clay. Almost all ceramic artists who work with pattern and texture accumulate a collection of texture-making items with which they then create a personal repertoire of decorative effects.

MATERIALS

Clay: equal quantities of molochite and powdered
white stoneware clay, plus 1 cup approx. of paper
pulp to every 1.5kg (3lb) of dry clay

Stains: Persian green, apple green, chrome green,
turquoise

Textured materials: string vest, lace,
embossed fabric

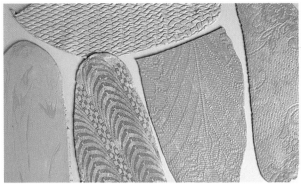

one Sheets of coloured and textured clays are
prepared in Persian green, apple green,
chrome green and turquoise. The
landscape textures are made from lace,
string vest and embossed fabrics; the sky is
marbled white and greens. It is important
that the sheets are all rolled out to the
same thickness.

two Two rectangles, each slightly larger than
the vase, are drawn adjacent to each other
on a piece of hessian or sacking placed on
a wooden board. These represent the two
sides of the vessel. A simple drawing of the
landscape is made on the hessian to act as
a guide for the clay pieces. Starting with
the sky, the landscape is built up from
pieces of the patterned sheets.

three For the distant hills, an interlocking piece
of textured clay is cut and fitted into the
sky shape. The landscape is then built up
from cut and torn shapes, with the pieces
fitting next to one another rather like a
jigsaw puzzle. The edges of the pieces are
pressed firmly together.

four

The clay landscape is lightly rolled, then turned over by placing a second wooden board on to the clay and flipping the work between the two boards. The hessian backing is peeled off to reveal the reverse side of the design. The reverse side of the clay is then welded by smoothing it with a metal kidney.

five

Using a potter's knife, the design is cut into two equal pieces. Each piece is laid carefully in a half of the mould, with the sky at the top of the vessel. Using a damp sponge, the clay is smoothed and pressed quickly into the mould before it starts to dry and lose its flexibility.

MAKING TECHNIQUE

Coloured clay with paper pulp

Paper pulp is quite simple to make. The more absorbent the paper, the more effective it is. Blotting paper is excellent; hard, shiny papers are not absorbent and should not be used.

To make paper pulp, tear or shred the paper into small pieces and leave them to soak in warm water until they are soggy. Put the mixture through a blender to break down the fibres of the paper. For immediate use, mix the paper pulp with wet clay. For storage, squeeze out the water and freeze until you need it. Paper pulp burns away completely during firing without affecting the finished vessel.

Clay bodies can be stained with commercial stains or colouring oxides and strengthened with paper pulp. The percentage of colouring substance can vary from 0.5 to 15 per cent or more, depending on the strength of the pigment and the colour required. For the landscape vase, the dry pigment amounted to around 5 per cent of the weight of the dry clay and molochite.

Mix the powdered clay and molochite with water to the consistency of very thick cream, using an electric mixer. When it is absolutely smooth, add the paper pulp and blend the mixture until any lumps have disappeared. Dissolve the pigment stain in a little boiling water and stir into the mixture.

Pour and spread the mixture on to a plaster slab to absorb excess moisture. When the coloured clay is stiff enough, remove it from the slab, ready for use.

DECORATING TECHNIQUE 1

Marbling clay

Two or more coloured clays can be kneaded together to make an effective marbled texture. Three different greens and white are used in this demonstration.

Build up slices of coloured clay to form a thick sandwich. Knead the clay sandwich a little to disperse the colours – the more it is kneaded, the finer the marbled pattern will be.

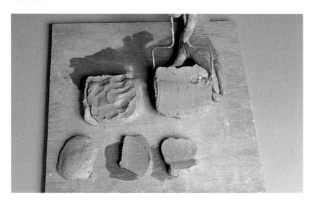

Finally, slice the kneaded clay to reveal the marbled pattern. If necessary, the slices can then be rolled to the required thickness.

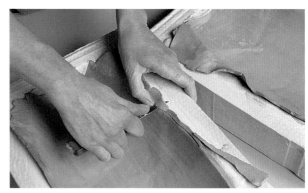

six Excess clay is trimmed with a potter's knife held parallel to the edge of the mould. The edges of the vase are scored and the base of the vessel is cut using a pastry cutter and then divided in two. The edges of the base are scored, painted with slip, and pressed into place in the mould.

seven The trimmed, scored edges are painted with slip and the mould put together. A small coil is smoothed into place on the inside seam to ensure a firm join (see Making technique on page 63).

eight When the clay is leather hard, the mould is opened and the vessel is lifted out. It is important to support the vessel from the inside during removal.

nine   Excess clay is removed from the join using a potter's knife, taking care not to alter the contour of the vessel.

DECORATING TECHNIQUE 2

Rolled textures

Lace, netting or any other material with an open texture can be rolled into slabs of wet clay to create a textured impression.

Lay a piece of lace on a thick slab of clay and then roll the clay to the required thickness.

Sponge a contrasting coloured slip on to the rolled fabric.

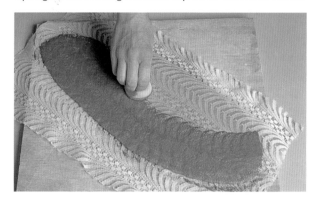

Finally, lift the fabric carefully to reveal the embossed, textured pattern underneath.

ten   Finally, the joins and the top edge are smoothed by wiping with a damp sponge. The vase is allowed to dry gradually before being once fired very slowly to 1200°C.

textured bowl

A ceramic patchwork is how artist Pollie Uttley describes her press-moulded bowl. She starts with a selection of patterned paper shapes cut mainly from anaglypta and other textured wallpapers. These pieces are then arranged and stuck on to sugar paper with rubberized glue, which transforms the paper collage into a flexible sheet. This simple mould gives a shallow relief pattern which is the standard starting point for most of Pollie's bowls.

From this common starting point, every bowl develops differently as the artist builds texture on texture, pattern on pattern. Motifs are taken from many sources including embroidery, lace, jewellery, metal letters and wooden printing blocks.

The patchwork idea came from the fabrics of Rajhastan and Gujurat discovered during Pollie's many trips to India. There she saw how the Indian women sewed old bodices and other discarded materials to make patchwork cushions and bedspreads, which were then overdyed in one colour. The same idea is used in Pollie's bowls.

MATERIALS

White earthenware clay

Textured fabrics and papers

Sugar paper

Rubberized glue

Piece of muslin

Household emulsion

Gilding powder

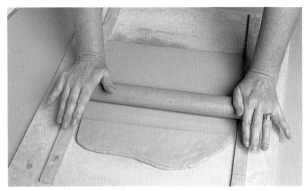

one The clay is rolled to the approximate shape of the envisaged bowl, though slightly larger all round.

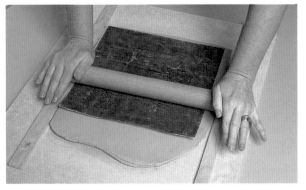

two A patchwork of textured fabrics and papers is arranged and stuck down on a sheet of sugar paper with rubberized glue. It is then pressed down on the sheet of clay and rolled firmly; the shallow texture of the embossed paper patterns forms the basis for further texture-making and imprinted motifs.

three The clay and textured paper is turned over and a piece of muslin pressed on to the reverse side of the clay and smoothed down. This is done to prevent the clay stretching and sticking.

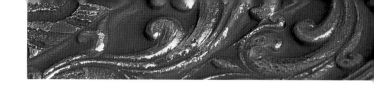

four The clay slab is carefully flipped over so that the muslin backing is underneath and the textured paper on top. The paper is peeled off carefully – if the clay is too wet, this can be tricky. The edges of the bowl are marked with a clay spike.

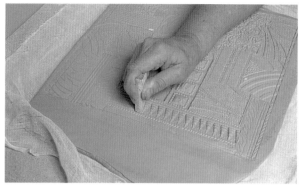

five Various raised patterns are stamped into the existing design using sprig moulds of earrings, buttons and cord.

six A textured mould made from a wooden Indian printing block is used to create a deep and elaborate leaf design.

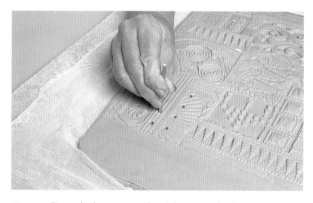

seven Deep holes are made with a metal tube (a drinking straw could be used instead), taking care not to puncture the reverse side of the clay. Gold thread can be laced through the holes when the bowl is complete, if required.

eight

A paper template the size of the press mould is laid on the clay slab, which is trimmed to fit with a potter's knife.

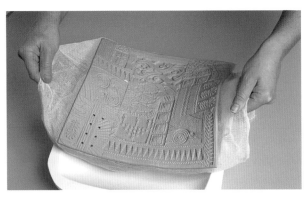

nine

The edges of the clay are softened with a damp sponge. This is done with a gentle up and down dabbing motion so as not to wipe away the design. Using the muslin backing as a sling, the clay slab is lifted up and placed centrally in the plaster mould.

ten

The clay is pressed gently into the centre of the mould and smoothed with the palm of the hand. Great care is taken not to spoil the printed patterns. The corners are pressed down with a dry sponge. Folded tissue is used to protect the pattern and a heavy weight is placed in the centre of the bowl. If this is not done, the bowl tends to flatten out as it dries. When dry, the bowl is biscuit fired to 1165°C.

eleven

The biscuit-fired bowl is painted with household emulsion using a small decorating brush. A light sponging removes some of the colour from the raised pattern, which is then brushed with bronzing powder (see Decorating technique on page 110).

DECORATING TECHNIQUE

Making a clay sprig mould

The sprig moulds which are used for many of the raised patterns on this bowl can be made quite simply from clay.

Start by rolling the clay into a thick slab. Press the earring, button or whatever object you are using firmly into the wet clay and then remove it to reveal the indented pattern. With buttons and earrings, a hairpin or loop of wire threaded through the button holes or clip makes it easier to lift the object from the clay.

Cut the patterned clay into manageable blocks using a long-bladed knife.

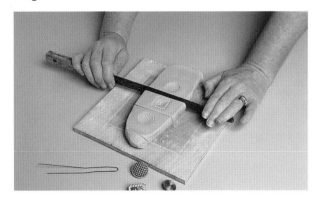

When the blocks are dry, fire them to a temperature of 1165°C. You now have a set of durable sprig moulds.

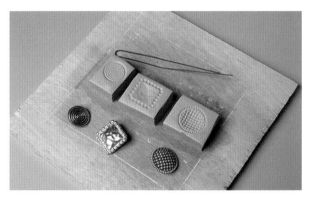

These are used by pressing a little clay into the block and then stamping the clay detail on to a slightly harder clay surface.

A detail of the bowl surface shows patterns made with embossed wallpaper, printing blocks, earrings, buttons, lace and an Indian amulet.

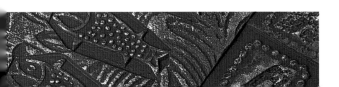

pear slab dish

Josie Walter is known mainly for her functional earthenware pots and distinctive slip decoration. Her approach is often painterly, the results lively and spontaneous. Over the years she has experimented with various decorative techniques including cut-and-torn paper resist, sgraffiti, spattering and slip trailing.

As with all her work, this piece explores the qualities inherent in the materials. The white slip on the dish is applied freely and quickly, allowing the earthenware body to show through. Thick, swirling brush strokes describe the pear's shape, while spattered texture and sgrafitto lines create a sense of movement and freshness.

For her slabbed pots, including this dish and the modelled spoon holder on page 92, Josie uses a coarse red sculpting clay. She finds this good for hand-building and likes its warm, mellow colour.

The work is once fired: in other words, there is no biscuit firing. The pots are glazed when leather hard, allowed to dry, and then fired to earthenware temperature.

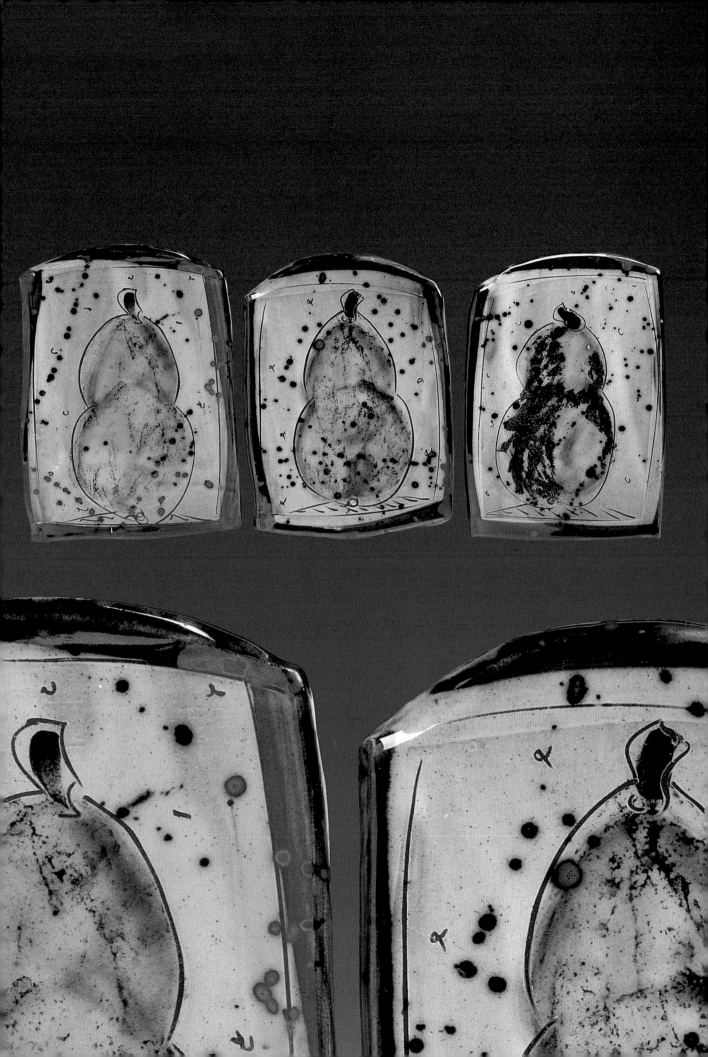

MATERIALS

Red earthenware sculpting clay

Wax resist

White slip made from Hyplas ball clay

Pale green slip made from Hyplas ball clay,
    plus 3% copper oxide

Brown slip made from red powder clay,
    plus 8% manganese

Dark green slip made from 2 parts copper oxide,
    1 part cobalt, 1 part ilmenite

Glaze: 10% red clay, 10% potash felspar, 75% lead
    basilicate, 5% borax frit, plus 4% bentonite

MAKING TECHNIQUE

Rims and edges

The edge or rim of your pots may be chunky or delicate, plain or patterned. There are lots of styles to choose from. But whatever your decision, the edge or rim defines the shape of a pot and also helps to determine its character.

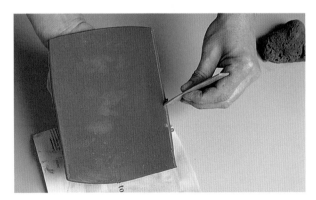

A notched stick used on the rim of a pot ensures an even finish. Here a wooden stick with a rounded notch is dragged around the cut edge of the dish clay.

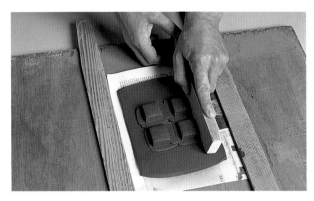

one A piece of soft clay is rolled and cut slightly larger than the intended dish. Although almost rectangular, the clay is cut freehand with shallow curved sides. A slightly thicker slab of clay is rolled for the feet, which are cut out as four squares. The clay for the dish is placed on newspaper and rolled lightly to elongate the shape and soften the edges. The feet are placed in position and flattened with a wooden batten, which is also used to press grooves between.

two The dish is picked up using the newspaper and laid over a roofing tile to create a curved form. It is then pressed down gently using a piece of wood.

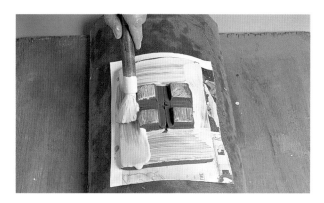

three The undersides of the feet are waxed to resist subsequent slips and glazes and left to dry. Thick white slip is applied to the underside of the dish. This is done in loose strokes with a pastry brush, allowing the red clay to show through the brush marks.

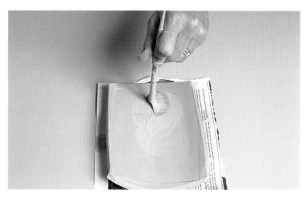

four When the dish is leather hard, the sharp edges are rounded with a piece of notched wood before being smoothed with a damp sponge. When the slip on the underside of the dish is dry, the white slip is poured over the inside of the dish and the excess removed from the edges with a finger. The pear is painted with pale green slip by twisting the vertically held brush to create swirling strokes which leave prominent ridges of thick slip.

five Brown slip is used for the stem and to sponge the textured shading on to one side of the pear, using a small piece of synthetic sponge. The edge of the dish is painted with dark green slip and sgraffito lines are scratched around the pear and background using a knitting needle, revealing the colour of the red clay underneath.

six The dish is spattered with dark green. This is done by loading a small brush and flicking the colour briskly across the surface design. Finally, the leather-hard vessel is dipped in glaze and when dry is once fired to 1080°C.

fish spoon holder

Although similar in construction to the dish in the previous project, this fish spoon holder has modelled details which give it an unusual sculptured appearance. The fins and other features on the fish are made from pieces of soft clay, which are pushed quickly and freshly into place with a wooden ruler to create a variety of surface patterns and textures. Because the clay is so soft there is no need to use water, which would detract from the fresh crispness of the modelled clay.

A paper template was used to cut the shape of this and similar pieces. The ridged feet on the base of the spoon holder are also cut from a paper template. Josie Walter, who designed and made the spoon holder, uses templates a lot, mostly for decorating but occasionally, as in this project, for cutting a shape from the clay. Like this fish design, many of her templates are abstracted or simplified versions of living creatures.

Although she says she finds it hard to use conventional art materials, preferring clay slip and a knitting needle to paints and pencils, drawing and painting skills play an important role in Josie's work. The lines and colours are bold and minimal, and the success of her designs is due in part to their freshness – and to her knowing exactly when to stop.

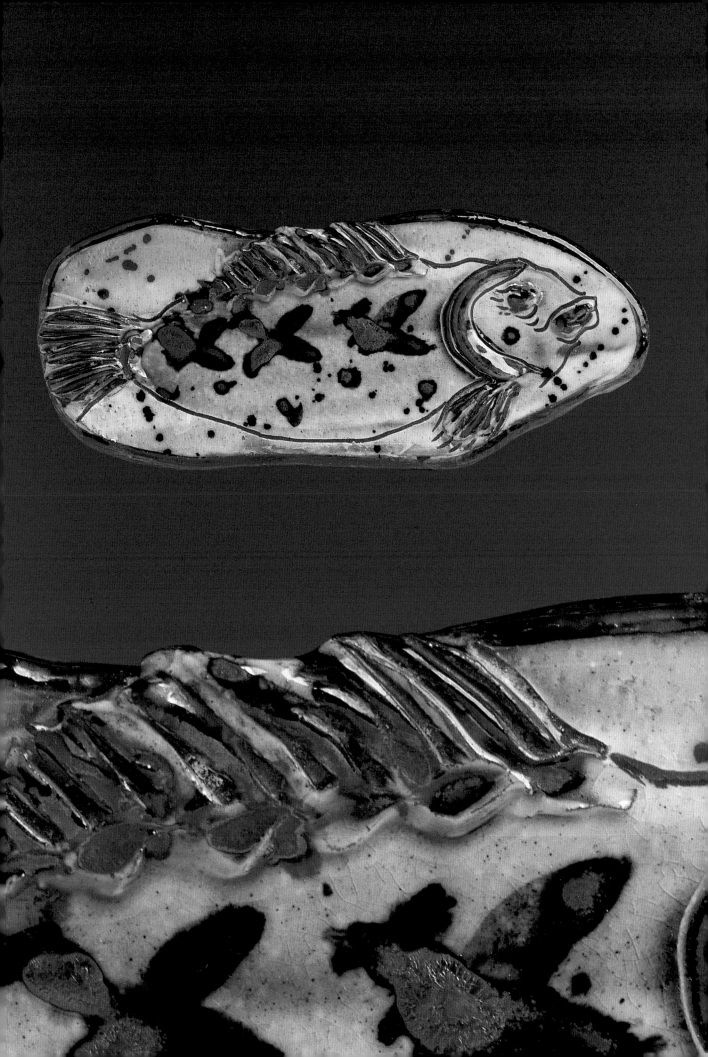

MATERIALS

Florist's wrapping paper (for templates)

Red earthenware sculpting clay

Wax resist

White slip made from Hyplas ball clay

Pale green slip made from Hyplas ball clay,
    plus 3% copper

Dark green slip made from 2 parts copper oxide, 1 part
    cobalt, 1 part ilmenite

Glaze: 10% red clay, 10% potash feldspar, 75% lead
    basilicate, 5% borax frit, plus 4% bentonite

DECORATING TECHNIQUE

Making templates

A template enables you to work out your design on paper before committing it to clay. It also allows you to produce a number of pieces with exactly the same decoration. Most papers can only be used once before the wet clay causes them to disintegrate, but Josie Walter has found that florist's wrapping paper makes a permanent template which can be washed in warm water after use and re-used over and over again.

You can make templates for details as well as for large shapes and decorations. For example, in this project paper templates were cut for the spoon holder shape and for the four feet.

Well-used templates made from florist's wrapping paper can be kept for future use, stored flat between the pages of a book.

one The clay is rolled out and the fish shape cut from a template. The feet are four bars of clay cut from a template, laid on the clay shape and joined by pressing with a narrow piece of wood to form three grooves. These are partly decorative – a device for making the bars of clay more interesting.

two The spoon holder is laid over a bottle until leather hard. The feet are then waxed to resist subsequent slips and glazes, and white slip is painted on the bottom of the spoon holder. When the slip on the reverse side is no longer tacky, the spoon holder is turned and the edges finished. It is now ready to be decorated.

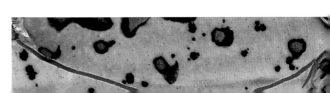

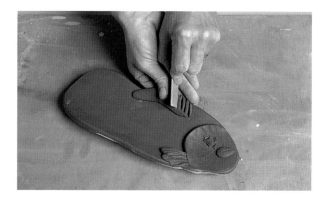

three The gill fins are small knobs of clay, laid in position and cut into using a piece of a broken wooden ruler; the gills are made from a sausage of clay pressed down and blended in on one side. A knob of flattened clay represents the eye, and the dorsal fins are a band of soft clay impressed with diagonal marks. This is underlined with a bold zigzag done with the finger.

four The tail is a fan-shaped piece of clay decorated with ridges impressed with a piece of wood.

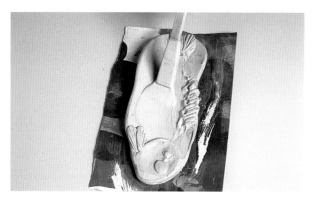

five White slip is poured over the front of the spoon holder. This acts as a base for the decoration and also helps the modelled clay to adhere more firmly to the main form. When this is dry, pale green slip is painted on to the body, head and fins with a hake brush.

six Dark green slip is painted around the edge and on the fins, and crosses are added. The same colour is then spattered over the surface. Irregular sgraffito lines, made with a knitting needle, loosely outline the fish's shape and add final decoration. The leather-hard spoon holder is dipped in glaze and once fired to 1080°C.

decorated bird tile

The warm colour of a quarry tile provides the perfect background for this bird painting. Maggie Angus Berkowitz uses similar tiles when she designs entire ceramic floors. Each tile is slightly different in tone and colour, so she lays out the whole floor area before starting the design, making sure that the irregular light and dark areas on the tiles are arranged in a harmonious way.

Two white glazes were used on the bird – a tin glaze because Maggie likes the way the iron and other oxides present in the red quarry tiles can affect the glazes, and a zircon glaze. The border of the tile is painted with a commercially prepared earthenware lustre glaze.

The drawing on this tile painting is done with a spirit-based pen – an unusual resist technique which gives the design an attractively sharp outline.

MATERIALS

20cm (8in) square quarry tile

Charcoal

Broad-tipped, spirit-based marker pen

Potterycraft white zircon glaze 2033

Potterycraft cinder-blue earthenware glaze

Bright red earthenware glaze

Pewter lustre glaze

DECORATING TECHNIQUE

Marker resist

An unusual resist effect can be achieved using a spirit-based marker, such as the Pentel 50. The marks resist the glaze, creating a bold, linear design which is very different from the effect achieved by the more traditional wax and latex resist methods.

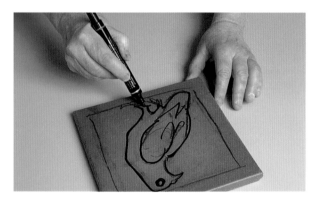

The marker technique is particularly useful on quarry tiles, because these have already been glazed to vitrification so that glazes applied to the hard surface cannot be absorbed. However, the marker defines and holds the shape of the glazed area and prevents the glaze from running.

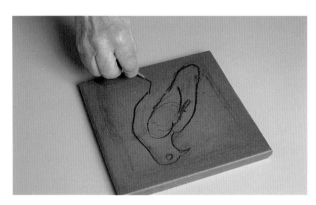

one The design is sketched out in charcoal – a deliberately bold, simple image to suit the broad, chunky lines of the marker pen.

two The main lines are overdrawn with a spirit-based marker. The border is sketched in as two parallel lines – these will form the edges of the glazed border to give an attractive cut-out effect. Areas to be painted are then dampened (this helps the glazes to spread on the non-porous surface of the already-glazed quarry tile). Using a large brush, white zircon glaze is flooded on to the bird.

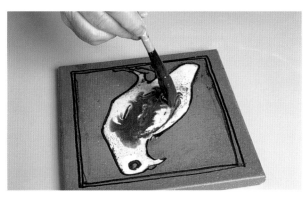

three The blue glaze is flooded into the centre of the bird, finding its own shape on the white. The eye is dotted in with bright red earthenware glaze.

four The border is painted with pewter lustre; the pen lines prevent the glaze from spreading and produce a fine, sharp outline. Finally, the bird's feet are dotted in with bright red earthenware glaze and the tile is fired to 1060°–1080°C with a five-minute soak.

DECORATING TECHNIQUE

Keeping a sketchbook

It is an excellent idea to carry a small pocket-sized sketchbook with you at all times. Take every chance to make sketches and visual notes of anything which catches your imagination. This way, you will always have a fund of ideas and inspiration at your fingertips. Depending on the subject, you may have to work quickly – especially when capturing people and moving creatures. However, this sense of urgency will certainly pay off, resulting in lively, spontaneous images which can then be incorporated into ceramic design and decoration.

Your drawing need not be confined to pencil or black and white: almost any medium is suitable for rapid, on-the-spot drawing and painting, including watercolour, gouache, coloured pencils, crayons and ink.

tiled panel

When working on her decorated earthenware tiles, Maggie Angus Berkowitz is as much a painter as she is a potter. The glaze designs are developed from her own drawings and sketches, and the figures and animals which play a central role in her work owe as much to the artist's knowledge of drawing, tone and colour as to her skill with clay and glazes.

The tiles are painted in various white glazes, all of which react differently with the transparent green glaze which is eventually poured over the whole tile. Each glaze is applied freely; the direction of the brush strokes, for example, is used to suggest swirling water, and the rounded form of the figures is described by varying the thickness of the tin glaze.

The figures are painted with a white tin glaze that reacts with the green glaze to produce a pinkish flesh colour. All the white glazes are applied to the water surface – the white zircon glaze creates the appearance of thick froth on some of the water. Before applying the overall green glaze, those unsubmerged parts of the figures are painted with a wax resist which protects them from the green and retains their pale flesh colour.

Although the fired glazes look entirely different from the pale powdery glazes as they are applied to the biscuit tiles, Maggie knows from experience how the colours will look when fired. She can also visualize the eventual tones and textures of her painted glazes, and makes copious glaze tests to find out which glaze combinations work together and which do not.

MATERIALS

Six 15cm (6in) white biscuit tiles

Charcoal

Tube lining in black and white

Slip trailer

Sneyd Oxides opacified white tin earthenware glaze

Sneyd Oxides lime matt glaze

Potterycraft white zinc earthenware glaze 2024

Potterycraft white zircon earthenware glaze 2033

Green earthenware glaze: 83% lead sesquisilicate,
8% feldspar, 6% china clay, 3% flint, plus 3%
whiting, 8% zinc oxide, 1.5% copper oxide (for
pouring) or 5% (for painting)

Wax resist

Pewter lustre glaze

DECORATING TECHNIQUE

Tube lining

A tile design can be outlined with slip or a mixture of
glaze and slip. The tube-lined tile is fired to a low
temperature and the glazes are then painted and
flooded into the areas between the raised lines.

In this demonstration, the tube lining is done with a slip
trailer. However, an eye dropper and even veterinary needles
can also be used, depending on the type of line required.

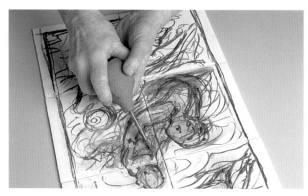

one A damp cloth or sponge is used to remove any
surface dust from the blank biscuit-fired tiles before
the design is drawn freehand in charcoal. Heavy
lines and excess charcoal dust are not a problem as
they will burn off during firing. The outline of the
drawing is defined by tube lining with a mixture of
glaze and slip, piped in a single line using a slip
trailer – the swimmers in black, the ripples on the
water in white. Where a figure is below water, the
slip-trailed water pattern is taken over it.

two The tiles are then fired to 850°C to adhere the tube
lining to the tile. Excess dust is wiped off the fired tile
with a damp sponge. Following the tube-lining
guide, a large hake brush is used to apply opacified
tin glaze to the swimmers. The patterns on the water
are filled in with three white glazes: zinc, zircon and
opacified tin. The lime matt glaze will be touched
with pink blushes after firing.

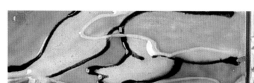

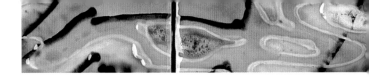

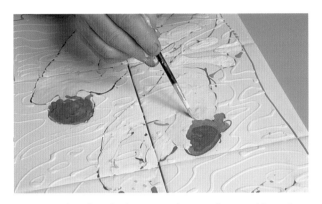

three Hair colour is the same glaze as that used later for the green water, but with 9 per cent iron substituted for the copper and the zinc. Wax resist is painted on to those parts of the swimmers which are out of the water – the wax masks the flesh colours from the subsequent green glaze. A little white zircon glaze is blobbed into the centre of selected water shapes – these areas will go frothy under the green and look like foam on the fired tile.

four A transparent pale green glaze is poured over each tile. To do this, the tile is gripped from the back and held almost vertically, with the border areas of the tile at the top. Fingertips are kept well back so as not to impede the glaze, which is poured steadily over the tile from a jug. Excess glaze is gently shaken from the tile, revealing the waxed areas which have resisted the glaze.

five Any glaze on the back of the tile and on the border area on the tile front is removed first by scraping, then by wiping. Darker areas of the water are painted with the transparent green glaze, but with 5 per cent of added copper instead of the original 1.5 per cent. This darker colour is dripped on from a well-loaded brush.

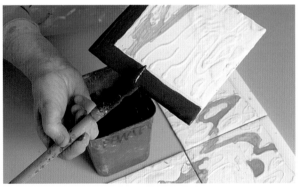

six A pewter lustre glaze is applied to the border areas with the hake brush. For a neat finish, the glaze is taken over the outside edges of each tile. Finally, the tiles are placed in a tile rack and fired at 1060°–1080°C with a five-minute soak. NOTE The tiles are loaded from the top of the rack to avoid bits of glaze and dust falling on to the tiles underneath.

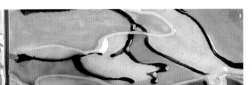

fish dish

Kirsti Fattorini makes strong, practical pots which can be used for cooking and for serving food. However, she also likes to decorate her functional stoneware with colourful, painted designs. Favourite sources of inspiration for these decorations include folk and Islamic art, animals and birds, and her own sketches.

Stoneware glazes are traditionally more subdued than earthenware glazes, but Kirsti makes the most of her stoneware palette. She applies glazes with a brush as if she were using paint, overlaying and mixing her colours to achieve precise tones and effects. Unlike many potters, she works with an extensive range of colours – seven different stoneware glazes are used on this fish dish. However, neutral oatmeal glazes form the basis of her colour schemes and the brighter glazes show up to advantage against this tonal base.

This fish dish was made from liquid clay slip poured into a plaster mould. This particular mould was made for Kirsti from a large oval baking dish, but she makes many of her moulds herself.

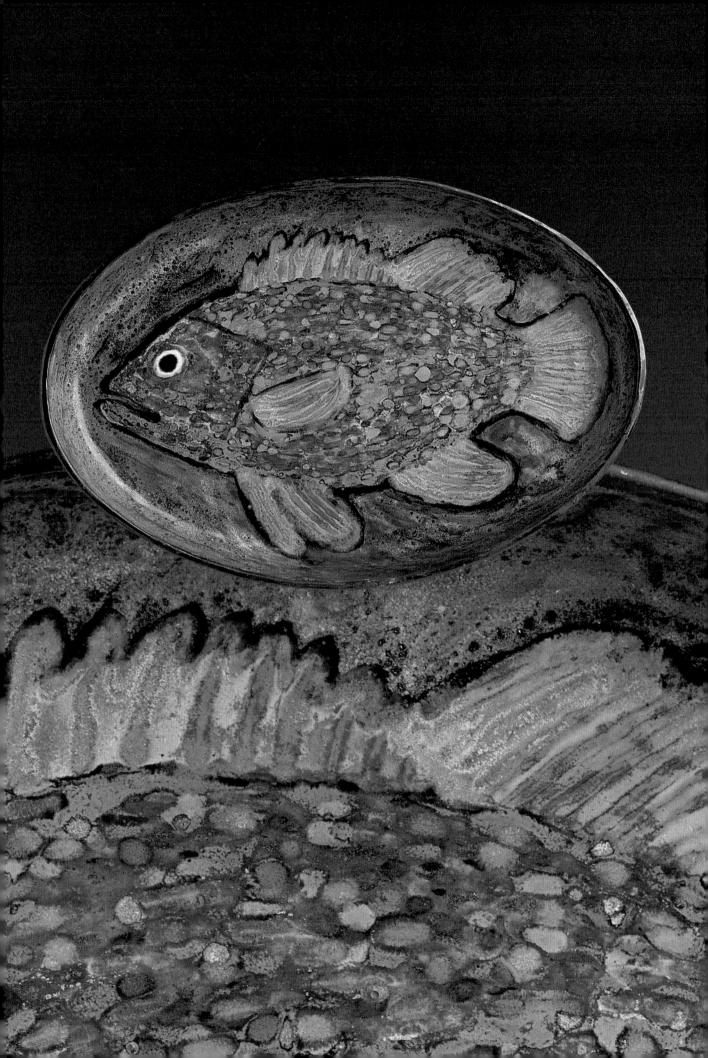

MATERIALS

Powdered stoneware clay

Potterycraft stoneware glazes: dark brown gloss,
    blue-grey, iron chun, light oatmeal, dark oatmeal,
    copper chun, fjord blue

Cobalt oxide

Wax resist

MAKING TECHNIQUE

Slip moulding

To make the dish, pour the casting slip through a sieve
into a plaster mould and leave for about an hour (smaller,
thinner pots need less time, depending on the thickness
required). As the water from the slip is absorbed into the
plaster, a deposit of solid clay builds up on the inside of the
mould to form the clay vessel. NOTE The casting slip used
here is mixed from powdered stoneware clay and water to
the consistency of single cream. Alternatively, the slip can
be bought ready mixed from a ceramic supply shop.

When the edges of the vessel are thick enough, the excess
slip is poured off. Leave the clay dish in the mould until it
has shrunk a little, then trim the rim with a fettling knife.
As it dries, the dish shrinks slightly and can be lifted easily
from the plaster mould. When leather hard, finish the rim
with a surformer and fire the dried dish to 950°C.

one A simplified design is drawn on to the biscuit-fired
dish with an ordinary pencil. The shape of the
motif is important and is chosen to suit the shape
of the dish; the fish motif fits perfectly into the
oval shape. Starting with the outline of the fish,
the background is painted with Potterycraft dark
brown gloss glaze. Two or three layers of the glaze
are applied with a well-loaded oriental brush,
allowing the glaze to run off the tip. The glaze is
at its thickest around the edge of the fish and near
the rim of the dish.

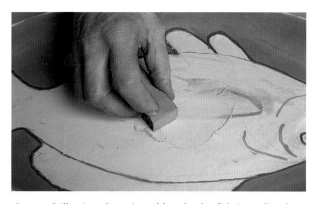

two Still using the oriental brush, the fish is outlined
with wax resist, taking the wax slightly over the
edge of the brown glaze. Mistakes made with the
wax resist are scraped off with a scalpel blade;
small unwanted patches of glaze are removed by
rubbing with an abrasive block or scouring pad.

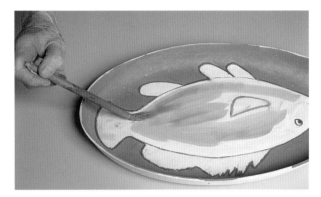

three The outlines of the fins are painted lightly with blue-grey glaze over cobalt oxide, then overpainted with iron chun glaze to produce a bright blue. Wax resist is painted over the outlines and left to dry. Light oatmeal glaze is painted along the top side of the fish and on the tail. Horizontal strokes of thick colour follow the body contours and help to describe its form. Still working in thick horizontal strokes, a dark oatmeal glaze is painted over the rest of the fish.

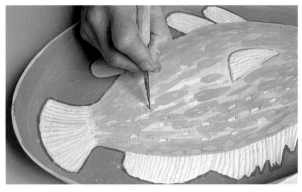

four Thick, parallel strokes of copper chun glaze are painted on to the fins and tail. The wax resist on the outline helps to define these lines. Fine stripes of fjord blue are painted with the tip of the brush over other glazes on the fins. Strokes of blue-grey glaze and blue-grey with added cobalt are built up in layers. The scales are dabbed on in iron chun glaze. To vary the thickness of the colour, flecks of glaze are scraped away to reveal the underlying clay.

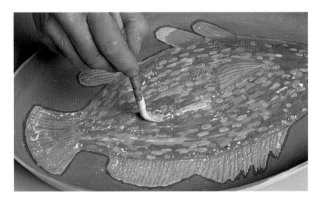

five Dabs of fjord blue are painted on to some of the scratched-out patches (this particular glaze looks good on biscuit but loses its colour when painted on top of oatmeal glazes). Other scratched areas are filled with white glaze and then painted over with copper chun to create light, bright spots of tone. More scales are painted in iron chun, copper chun and blue-grey, and the fish is painted with wax using broad, horizontal strokes.

six Blue-grey glaze is poured over the whole interior of the dish and then quickly poured off, leaving the waxed area that is protected from the glaze. The rim is painted in the blue-grey with added cobalt and an overpainting of iron chun glaze, the outside of the dish in glossy brown with a coat of blue-grey on top. Finally, any flecks of remaining glaze on the waxed fish are wiped off with a sponge and the dish is fired to 1250°C.

temple
mirror frame

These unusual ceramic temple mirrors were inspired by the architecture and textiles of India. As well as constantly recording what he saw during his many visits to that country, Garry Uttley also sought and saved anything which he felt could be used to create unusual textures and patterns in his work. His studio collection of decorating 'tools' currently includes printing blocks, engraver's letters and pieces of carved wood. Less exotic, but equally effective, are the cork fishing floats, discarded drinking straws and scraps of plastic bubblewrap that Garry also uses to embellish his frames.

Although the temple mirrors are built from sections of flat clay, their construction and heavy surface decoration combine to give them a three-dimensional appearance. The play of light and shadow on the decorated surface contributes to this effect and is an important part of the finished piece.

Two biscuit-fired moulds are used in the making of the temple frames: the first to create the bubblewrap texture of the decorative roof, the second to make the barley-sugar pillars at each side of the mirror. The latter are made by pressing wooden moulding into a block of clay.

Each frame is made and fired in two or more sections. The fired pieces are then decorated and assembled. Unlike most ceramics, these mirrors are not glazed. Instead, the biscuit-fired clay is painted with household emulsion and then enhanced by rubbing with gilding powder. The finished frame can be cleaned by wiping lightly with a damp cloth.

MATERIALS

White earthenware clay
Household emulsion paint
Gilding powder
Metallic paint medium

DECORATING TECHNIQUE

Gilding powder

Gilding powder is available in gold, silver, pewter and other metallic finishes from good art and craft suppliers and is very simple to use. The powder is usually mixed with a proprietary metallic paint medium, but make sure you always follow the manufacturer's instructions.

Mix the gilding powder with metallic paint medium to a creamy consistency, then brush the solution lightly over the raised areas of the painted frame using just the tip of the bristles.

one The clay is rolled and left overnight between flat boards. This allows it to stiffen slightly, making it easier to work. A template for the basic mirror shape is cut from card and the clay frame cut around this using a metal spike. A ruler is used to mark the position of the slanting roof; this line is then scored with a knife and painted with clay slip made from the earthenware clay body.

two A strip of clay the same thickness as the main mirror is cut for the underside of the roof. The outside edge is bevelled ready to receive the roof section. The strip is then fixed by pressing firmly along the scored, slipped area.

three The slanting roof section is cut, slightly thinner than the roof underside, and rolled over the biscuit-fired bubblewrap mould. The rolling is firm enough to create a clear impression, but not so hard that it cuts the clay. The textured clay is then lifted carefully to avoid stretching and cut to fit.

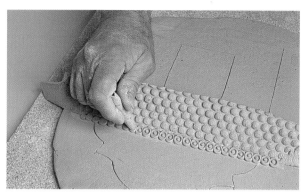

four The bevelled edge of the underside of the roof is scored and slipped, and the textured roof shape lifted into position. To disguise the join between the roof and the frame, small balls of clay are rolled, arranged along the top of the roof, and impressed with a cork fishing float.

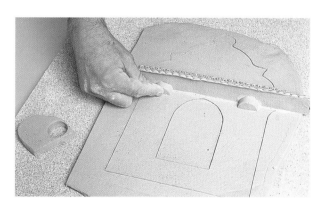

five For the tops of the pillars, a circle of clay is cut using a small glass or a pastry cutter and then cut in two. These semicircular pieces are then scored and stuck in position underneath the roof at each side of the mirror.

six Each barley-sugar pillar is formed from a sausage of clay. This is pressed into a biscuit-fired mould and the surplus removed using a metal kidney. The moulded clay is then removed carefully, so as to avoid any tearing or stretching.

MAKING TECHNIQUE

Texture mould

Bubblewrap, embossed paper and other similarly patterned and textured materials can be rolled or pressed into wet clay to create an effective impression. However, such materials are ephemeral and will eventually wear out or become clogged with clay and lose definition. In any case, they only create an indented, or negative, impression of a particular texture.

It is very simple to make a clay mould from any textured surface. When biscuit fired, this can be pressed on to wet clay to recreate an exact replica of the pattern or texture, and has the added advantage of being permanent, so it can be used over and over again.

The technique for making the mould is similar to that used for making the sprig mould on page 87. In this demonstration, a piece of bubblewrap is used to create the texture mould. Other possibilities include fabric, lace, netting and wire mesh.

Roll out a thick slab of clay and then roll the textured material into the wet clay. Remove the material carefully to reveal the patterned clay surface. Trim the edges to form a neat block, which is then fired to a temperature of 1165°C.

seven The pillars are scored and slipped, and stuck in position at each side of the mirror. Two matching semicircular clay pieces are then stuck at the bottom of each pillar (see step 5). Sprig decorations are applied to the top of the mirror and below the decorative roof.

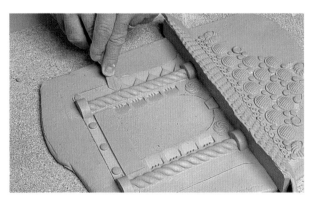

eight Further details are added to the frame, and a wooden modelling tool is used to impress faceted decoration on each side of the mirror. The edge is cut and trimmed, using a potter's knife held at right angles to the frame to ensure a square cut.

nine The bottom section of the frame consists of a flat back with a fixed shelf, both slightly wider than the main mirror piece. The shelf is supported with clay brackets to prevent warping. Embossed decorative texture is created using various carved printing blocks.

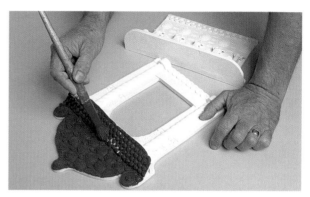

ten The two dried frame sections are fired to 1165°C and then painted with household emulsion diluted to the consistency of single cream. The porous, textured surface calls for a stippling motion rather than conventional brush strokes.

eleven Excess paint is sponged off the raised areas with a moist sponge – this produces graded colour with light and dark variations.

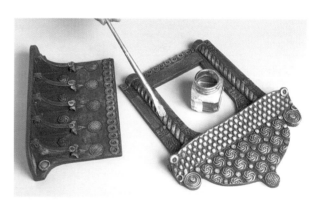

twelve Finally, the decoration is completed with a dusting of light gold gilding powder applied lightly over the base colour.

smoke-fired jug

This attractively flattened jug is made by joining two identical shapes which have been formed in a shallow press mould. Jacqui Atkin, who made this and the smoke-fired bottle in the following project, describes the jug and other flattened forms as having 'two-and-a-half dimensions'.

The mould is used for the body of the jug only. This allows the artist to use the same mould for different jug designs by varying the tops. These are made and added separately. Initially, the top of the jug is made as a symmetrical form, which is then shaped and cut to create the pouring spout.

A large coil forms a sturdy, stable base for the jug. Similar bases, using one or more coils, can be added to any press-moulded pot. However, correct proportions are important: it is easy to end up with a pot that is bottom-heavy.

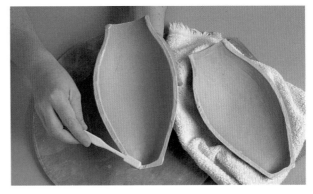

MATERIALS

Clay: 50% T-material, 50% porcelain

Green slip made from body clay, plus 5% green stain

Slurry made from crank clay and water

Beeswax polish

MAKING TECHNIQUE

Using two press-moulded pieces

The procedure for making a pot from two press-moulded pieces is exactly the same as that used for the press-moulded bowl on page 82, except that in this case you must make two pieces – one for each side of the pot. If you are making a symmetrical pot, the mould must also be symmetrical.

Important things to remember are that the clay for the two halves should be the same thickness, and that when joining them together they should be at the same stage of dryness.

Make two press-moulded shapes, taking care to trim the rim horizontally using a wooden tool. This makes it easier when joining the two together.

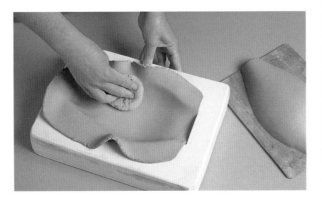

one The body of the jug is constructed from two press-moulded halves. Each piece is dried a little on the outside with a hairdryer, making it stiff enough to handle, and the two halves are joined together by scoring and wetting. The join is made carefully, because the neck of the jug is too narrow to add a supporting coil inside (see Making technique on page 63).

two A wooden spatula is used to smooth and improve the contours of the jug and to reinforce the joins.

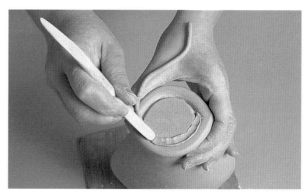

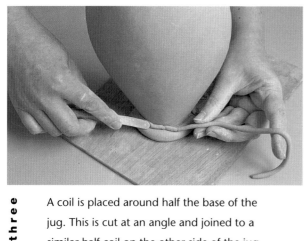

three A coil is placed around half the base of the jug. This is cut at an angle and joined to a similar half coil on the other side of the jug by scoring and wetting. A much smaller coil is rolled to fill the space between the jug and the coil. This is blended in using a wooden modelling tool.

four Another coil is used to fill the space on the base of the jug. This too is blended in using a wooden tool.

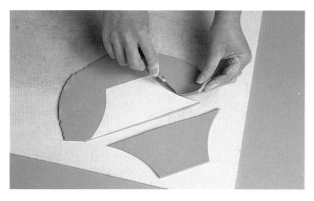

five For the top of the jug, a piece of clay is rolled to the same thickness as the body and two shapes are cut from a card template. At this stage, the top is deliberately too tall, to allow scope for shaping and cutting to a suitable size.

six The rim of the jug body is levelled and trimmed with a surformer ready to receive the top. The top section is constructed and fitted to the main body using the scoring and wetting technique (see Making technique on page 63). The joins are reinforced with small coils on both inside and outside. The top is then held in position and dried with a hairdryer until it is dry enough to support itself. The rim is shaped and trimmed with a craft knife.

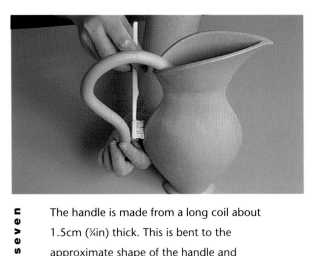

seven The handle is made from a long coil about 1.5cm (¾in) thick. This is bent to the approximate shape of the handle and allowed to stiffen slightly, at which point it is re-formed into a more precise shape and allowed to dry a little more. The handle is fixed on the inside of the jug by scoring and slipping, and held in position until slightly dry. The bottom of the handle is joined in a similar manner.

eight When leather hard, the jug is painted with green slip and burnished (see Decorating technique on page 75). When dry, it is biscuit fired to 950°C.

nine The biscuit-fired pot is decorated with masking tape, making sure the two sides are symmetrical.

ten A coat of thick paste, or slurry, mixed from crank clay and water is applied all over the patterned surface.

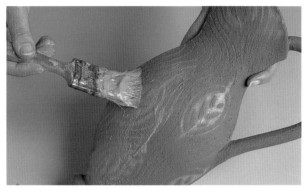

eleven Further coats of slurry are applied until the masking tape is completely covered. The slurry is allowed to dry and the pot warmed slightly to reduce the risk of cracking during firing. The jug is then placed in a sawdust kiln and fired according to the instructions given on pages 36–37.

DECORATING TECHNIQUE

Smoked patterns with masking tape

Beautiful black patterns can be created on a smoke-fired pot using masking tape covered with a very thick mixture, or slurry, of crank clay and water. When fired, the tape burns away under the slurry, leaving black carbonized marks on the pot.

For linear patterns, cut long narrow strips from a standard width of masking tape stuck down on a cutting board. You will need a sharp craft knife in order to get crisp edges. Use a ruler and keep the strips the same width by following the guidelines on the board. For wavy lines, pull the strips into shape as you stick them on the pot.

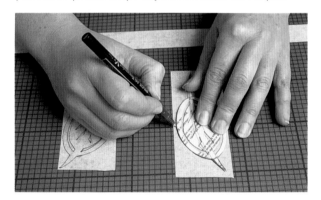

Use a template for shapes and patterns. Remember, on a symmetrical vessel like this jug, shapes must be reversed if the two sides are to look the same.

twelve When cool, the jug is taken from the sawdust kiln and the dried slurry removed, before washing the jug in warm water. The jug is then warmed slightly before being given two coats of beeswax polish.

Lift the tape and stick in position on the biscuit-fired pot. Cover the pot and masked patterns with slurry, and allow this to dry before smoke firing with newspaper or sawdust (see Smoke firing on pages 36–37).

coiled bottle

However carefully it is made, the walls of a coil pot are never completely even, the shape never quite symmetrical. Each pot is unique, and there are as many different ways of coiling a pot as there are potters who coil them.

Jacqui Atkin made this elegant bottle with large, flattened coils joined together with smaller, round coils. However, some artists prefer to work entirely with round coils, sometimes using very soft clay so that the coils can be blended together without the need for water or slip. Others like to use an extruder – a simple machine which forces clay through shaped holes to produce completely regular coils of the shape required.

Whatever the method, coiling is a slow, contemplative way of working. Ideally, the clay should be left to dry slightly between coils – a time-consuming process, even when speeded up with a hairdryer. The T-material in the clay used for this project creates an excellent body for coiling, because it dries evenly and does not readily dry out and crack at the edges as can happen with other clays.

On the downside, the molochite in T-material makes it too granular to burnish easily. The solution here is to make a slip of the body clay and pass this through a 100 mesh sieve to get rid of the molochite. This smooth slip is applied to the leather-hard vessel, which can then be burnished in the normal way.

MATERIALS

Clay: 50% T-material, 50% porcelain

Slip made from clay body and water, sieved

Slurry made from crank clay and water

Beeswax polish

MAKING TECHNIQUE

Making coils

Building a coil pot is much easier if the coils are properly made and of an even thickness. They can be either rounded or flattened, like the ones shown here. Alternatively, some potters develop their own coil types with cross-sections that are oval, wedge-shaped or even T-shaped.

Whichever type of coil you choose, start by pulling the clay into a thick sausage shape.

Roll the clay to the thickness you want using long, smooth movements. Use the flat of your hands, starting with your hands together and moving them apart as the coil gets longer. Give the coil an occasional twist to keep it even and compact.

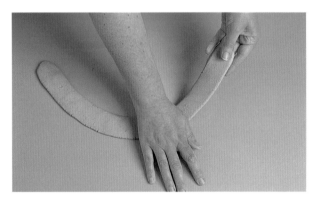

For a flattened coil, use a short chopping movement with the side of your hand. Work first on one side, then flip the coil and do the same on the other side. For curved pots, bend the coil as you flatten it – this will help you to build concave and convex forms.

one The base of the bottle is made by flattening a ball of clay with the flat of the hand. The round shape is then marked and cut out using a potter's knife. This process is carried out on a whirler to ensure a circular shape.

two The base is scored and slipped, and the first flattened coil is then put in place, with the shortest side around the base. The join is overlapped for extra strength and squeezed together. A wooden tool is used to blend the join and to join the base to the coil. A small, soft coil is worked into the inside of the base to reinforce it.

three A second flattened coil is added and pressed firmly into the rim of the first coil. It is important to stagger the joins of the coils so that they do not always occur in the same place, as this would cause a weakness in the vessel.

four A small round coil is rolled and blended into the join on the inside of the bottle.

five A similar coil is pressed into the outside join and blended in with a wooden modelling tool.

six This coil, and every subsequent one, is trimmed with a surformer before being scored and slipped ready to receive the next coil.

seven As the bottle starts to narrow, the longer (convex) edge of the curved coil is joined to the body. This causes the shape of the bottle to get narrower.

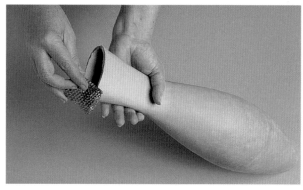

eight Straight coils are used for the top of the bottle, and these are pulled and manipulated into a flared shape. A surformer is used to straighten and tidy the rim. The sides and rim of the bottle are scraped and finished with a smooth kidney.

nine The bottle is then given three coats of white slip, made from the body clay sieved through a 100 mesh sieve. This is burnished, and the dried pot is then biscuit fired to 950°C. Thin strips of masking tape are cut to decorate the biscuit-fired bottle.

ten The decorated pot is then covered with a thick layer of slurry mixed from crank clay and water and allowed to dry.

eleven After smoke firing in newspaper (see Smoke firing on pages 36–37), the dried slurry is removed by peeling and chipping.

twelve The pot is then washed, dried and warmed before being polished with two coats of beeswax polish.

hump-moulded dish

These pretty dishes were made by placing a sheet of lace-textured clay over a hump mould. The technique is similar to press moulding, but instead of placing the rolled clay inside the mould it is laid on top and either cut or manipulated to fit. The mould used here is a biscuit-fired clay cone, but hump moulds are often made from plaster of Paris and other materials. Improvised hump moulds include any object with a convex surface, such as an existing bowl or dish or a block of wood.

An overlapping clay seam is an attractive but necessary feature of the design; a blended join would have spoiled the imprinted lacy texture on the inside of the dish – a feature which potter Tricia Evans wanted to preserve.

The conical shape of the dish is not self-supporting and is designed for use with a foot ring. This is added as a final stage, great care being taken to choose a ring of the right shape, weight and size.

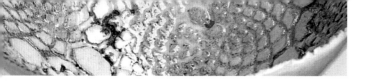

MATERIALS

Clay: 50% T-material, 50% porcelain

Piece of lace

Oxides for colouring

Potclays white dolomite stoneware glaze

one A piece of lace is placed on a sheet of clay and rolled evenly and firmly to imprint the lacy pattern on the clay. The lace is removed and the clay left to stiffen a little. NOTE Rolling on a sheet of plastic or fabric ensures the clay can be removed easily.

MAKING TECHNIQUE

Choosing a foot ring

A foot ring can be added easily to a hand-built pot, but it is important to choose the right one. It is all too easy to make the foot either very heavy or too small.

It is a good idea to make several foot rings and try them out to see which looks best on your pot. The spare ones can even be fired and kept, so that you have a permanent selection of different shapes and sizes from which to choose the ones that look best on your pots.

two The clay is turned over and lifted, patterned side down, on to the hump mould. To make the work portable and accessible at this stage, the mould is placed on a circular board. The position of the overlap is marked with a knife and the surplus clay is cut away, leaving a narrow margin of clay to make the overlapping seam.

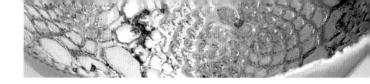

three The seam is joined by scoring and wetting, and then blending with the finger. The clay is smoothed by scraping down lightly with a metal kidney, taking care not to flatten the texture on the inside.

four Surplus clay is cut away from the rim using a sharp craft knife.

five The foot ring here is made from a flattened coil but could equally well be cut from rolled clay. This is then made into a circular foot ring and the surplus clay trimmed off. The seam is blended with a wooden tool. For a perfectly circular foot ring, the clay can be rolled around a former such as a rolling pin or tube.

six The foot ring and the base of the pot are scored and slipped. The foot ring is fixed in position with a small coil, which is then blended in. When dry, the pot is biscuit fired to 950°C. It is then sponged with a solution of oxides and water, before being dipped in white dolomite glaze. The pot is then fired to 1250°C.

vase with handles

Whether decorative or purely functional, handles can make all the difference to a pot. The main considerations are shape and size, but the position of the handles is also a crucial factor. Once fixed, the handles become an integral part of the pot and can either enhance or destroy the basic form.

The forerunner of modern handles were 'lugs' – compact protrusions used for holding and hanging many early pots. Although lug handles are still used both decoratively and for practical reasons – being compact and strong for casseroles and other ovenware – they have been largely replaced by handles which can be grasped by the whole hand.

Tricia Evans tried several different handles on her press-moulded vase before deciding on unusual scrolled coils for the finished pot. Because the vessel is a decorative piece, she felt free to choose ornamental handles and to place these where they looked best – with the tops virtually on a line with the rim of the vase. However, she points out that for functional pots, other factors should be considered. For example, mugs and cups require handles which can be held comfortably with the whole hand and hung easily from hooks when not in use.

The glaze recipes given here are for a white and turquoise glaze pattern, but the colours can be varied by using different coloured stains.

MATERIALS

Clay: 50% T-material, 50% porcelain

Wax resist

Turquoise stoneware glaze: 85% Cornish stone, 15%
    whiting, plus 2% bentonite, 7% turquoise stain

White stoneware glaze: 85% Cornish stone, 15%
    whiting, plus 2% bentonite, 4% tin

MAKING TECHNIQUE

Pots with handles

With hand-built pots, the handles are usually made
separately and then added to the pot. As you can see
from these examples, there are various possibilities.

 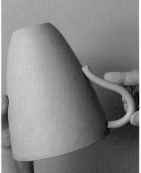

SLAB HANDLES

Handles can be cut from a slab of stiff or leather-hard clay.
Use a card template to get the handles exactly the same size.

COIL HANDLES

A classic handle can be made from a roll of clay.
Decorative versions include twisted, textured or even
plaited coils.

one Although shallow vessels are usually press
moulded from one rolled slab of clay, the deeper
mould used for this vase is easier to use with two
or more pieces of clay. Here, two rolled pieces are
pressed into the mould, with edges overlapping
by about 2.5cm (1in). The edges are pressed
together and a little more clay pressed into the
base of the vase for increased thickness and
stability. The inside of the vase is then scraped
and smoothed with a metal kidney.

two The surplus clay at the top of the vase is cut off
using a piece of wood, held parallel to the top
of the mould to ensure an even rim. The clay is
dried off slightly with a hairdryer, until it begins to
shrink from the side of the mould and can be
removed easily.

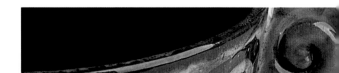

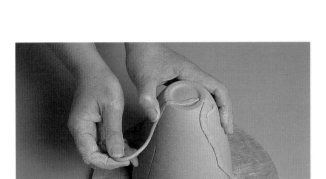

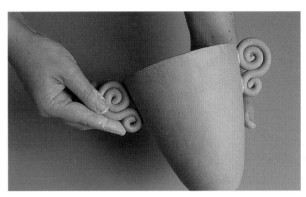

three The clay form is removed from the mould and small coils are pressed in to hide and strengthen the overlapped joins on the outside surface. A metal scraper is used to blend the coils and smooth the outside of the vase.

four The handles are made from coils of clay rolled into a double scroll design. When the handles are stiff enough to handle, they are fixed in position by scoring and slipping. It is important to judge the correct positioning of the second handle from all angles to ensure it is placed symmetrically with the first. The dried pot is then biscuit fired to 950°C.

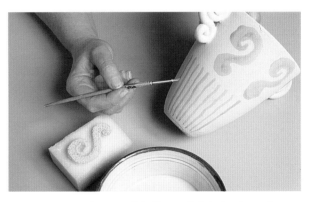

five The foot of the pot is painted with wax to protect the base from the glaze, which would otherwise stick to the kiln shelf during firing. The pot is then dipped in a turquoise stoneware glaze.

six Using a sharp craft knife, a relief design is cut from a piece of synthetic sponge. Here the pattern is designed to repeat the shape of the scroll handle. The sponge design is dipped in wax and pressed on to the pot to form a repeat pattern around the rim. Finally, some wax resist lines are painted on the lower half of the pot. When these are dry, white stoneware glaze is lightly sponged all over the outside of the pot, which is then fired to 1260°C.

garden sculpture

Rosie Bennell is a garden designer and a ceramic artist. Most of her work is inspired by natural forms, which are carefully studied and drawn. The drawings are developed and become more abstract and sculptural as she extracts and develops those elements she wants to incorporate in the finished piece. Preliminary models also play an important role in the design process.

Natural subject sources range from fruit and vegetables to bones and driftwood. The starting point for this project piece was the skeleton of a snake's head.

Because most of Rosie's work is destined for an open garden setting, it is important that the sculptures look equally good from whichever angle they are viewed. Rosie works from all sides, turning the sculpture frequently during construction so that she can assess the form from every viewpoint.

This coiled piece is one of the artist's smaller works. Some of her sculptures are much larger, but these are usually made and fired in two or more sections and then assembled on site. Each finished work is displayed out of doors on a solid base, such as stone or concrete. This avoids moisture from the soil being absorbed into the porous clay and so minimizes the risk of damage by frost. A hole in the base of each work is an additional protection against frost damage.

MATERIALS

Crank clay

Off-white slip

Beige slip, mixed from ball clay and water

Orange-tan slip, mixed from 5 parts ball clay
    and 1 part rutile

Black iron oxide mixed with water

Rutile, mixed with water and a small amount each
    of high-temperature borax frit and ball clay

one Working from drawings and a 1:2 scale model, the base is made from a thick slab of clay either rolled or flattened with the hand. Using a paper template as a guide, the position of the first coil is marked on the base. The coils are thick rolls of clay flattened slightly with the side of the hand, made in advance and left to stiffen slightly.

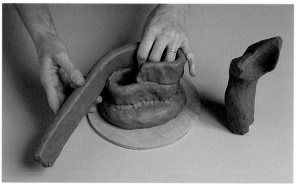

two Following the model as a guide, the first and second coils are added and blended with a modelling tool and fingers on the inside and outside. Depending on the shape desired, coils are placed either just on the inside or just on the outside of the existing coil to make the form wider or narrower.

three Still following the model as a guide, the walls are built up coil by coil. As the sculpture grows, a hairdryer or fan heater is used to stiffen and strengthen the form before each new coil is added. If the top edge does become dry, it is scored with a knife and dampened with water. If the work is left for a period, perhaps overnight, the top edge can be kept workable by wrapping it in cling film or a moist cloth.

four Contours and form are constantly assessed for accuracy using the model as a guide. A tape measure is kept to hand for checking the proportions of the full-scale sculpture. A wooden spoon or paddle is used to beat the form into shape.

five In the upper half of the sculpture, the form changes direction more dramatically and narrower coils are often used. Coils are added in small sections rather than complete rings. As shown here, some parts are built up before others.

MAKING TECHNIQUE

Models and sketches

Preliminary models and sketches are invaluable when working on large-scale pieces such as these garden forms. The sketches need contain very little detail – many working drawings are simply a guide to the overall shape of the finished piece – and your model can be much smaller than the anticipated work. Also, a preliminary model need not necessarily be made from clay, but can employ many other materials, including paper, cardboard, wood and metal.

Once the model is made, the full-sized piece can be made to scale. For example, the model used here is one half the size of the full-scale piece.

For a simple model, start with a piece of clay and mould this into the approximate form you want. Experiment with the shape and surface of the model, removing clay with a modelling tool and making additions and alterations where necessary.

These models, made by Rosie Bennell, are moulded from various types of clay.

NOTE Very solid clay forms may be too thick to fire, in which case they should be handled with care. Alternatively, hollow out the clay with a wire modelling tool and biscuit fire the model in the normal way.

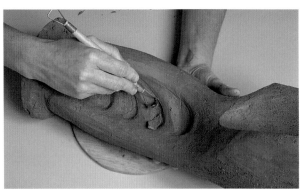

six The upper section is completed and the form closed off. During this latter construction stage the sculpture is stiffened frequently by drying slightly with a hairdryer to prevent subsequent coils from causing sagging (this is especially important as the form swells out, creating an overhang). When dry or stiff enough to handle, the form is scraped with a metal kidney to remove irregularities and define the edges.

seven While working on the surface, small amounts of fresh clay are added, either to build up badly defined edges or to fill in obvious depressions. Where the clay surface has become dry, it is scored and dampened before filling. A wire modelling tool is used to define the series of grooves in the recessed area. Great care is taken not to remove too much clay, as it is quite possible to scrape right through the wall of the sculpture during this process.

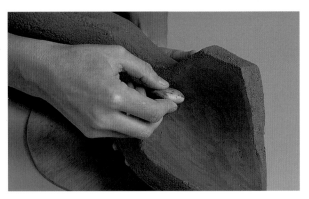

eight Once the form has been refined, textures can be added. Selected areas are burnished to create a smooth surface, in deliberate contrast to the coarser areas elsewhere on the work. Here a smooth pebble is used to polish the concave section of the sculpture.

nine Surface textures are built up using both smooth and rough kidneys. Scraping the surface of the coarse crank clay creates a rough texture, even when using a smooth kidney. A serrated kidney is used to create ridges and linear marks. Some deep textural ridges which accentuate the form of the top surface are created by scraping with a fork.

ten The solid clay base is hollowed out using a knife and modelling tools. This is necessary because a base which is so much thicker than the rest of the piece is liable to crack open during firing. During this process the sculpture is laid on pads of foam or fabric to protect the clay surface. Before firing, a hole is made in the base to allow air to escape during firing.

elevn Three slips – off-white, beige and an orange-tan – are applied to the leather-hard sculpture using a soft hake brush. Because it is important not to clog the textural grooves, the colour is picked up on the tips of the bristles and dragged lightly over the surface rather than completely covering the form with solid colour. The off-white slip is used mainly to emphasize the edges of the form.

twelve To contrast with the textural surface elsewhere, the smooth concave area is painted with two layers of thick beige slip and then burnished. Two layers of orange-tan slip are likewise painted on and burnished. The slipped sculpture is allowed to dry thoroughly and is biscuit fired to about 1000°C.

thirteen A strong solution of black iron oxide and water is sponged over the surface. This is a messy job, so strong rubber gloves should be worn. Excess is removed with a squeezed-out sponge, leaving oxides in the depressions to emphasize the surface textures. Finally, a wash of rutile and water mixed with a little borax frit is applied to the frontal depression to give a glowing orange-tan colour when fired. The sculpture is fired to about 1250°C.

SETTING UP A SMALL STUDIO

If you have a small room to spare, you have a potential pottery studio. The other initial requirements are electricity for the kiln, plus a water supply and sink. True, a few potters manage without water in the studio itself, and do their washing up and mixing outside or at another indoor tap. But working with clay and glazes without running water close at hand can be a nightmare and is not a serious possibility except in an emergency or the very short term.

Daylight is pleasant to work by, but by no means essential. Many potters work in a converted cellar, which is fine provided it is dry, has good artificial lighting and provides adequate ventilation for both you and the kiln.

Wherever the studio, the floor should be washable and not covered with any material that harbours dust.

PLANNING THE SPACE

Planning a studio without having first worked in the allocated space and discovered what is needed and where it should go is not easy. As this is something of a chicken-and-egg situation, a good compromise is to start with the minimum amount of furniture and equipment and add to this as the needs arise. Probably the first essential item at this stage is a sturdy bench or table for working on and for preparing and rolling clay.

Because of the need for wiring and sockets, you will also have to make an early decision about positioning the kiln. This should be in a place where it can be properly ventilated and is not in the way. Depending on the type of kiln, remember to leave adequate surrounding space for access, ventilation and servicing.

DRAINAGE

A clay trap under the sink will stop the drains becoming clogged with clay and also prevent toxic materials getting into the drainage system. This is usually a simple set-up, whereby the waste water passes through a series of chambers in a plastic tank. Particles of clay and other waste materials are trapped and sink as sediment to the bottom of the chambers; the water that finally goes down the drain is relatively clean. Purchased clay traps are portable and can be wheeled out for easy emptying.

STORAGE

Ideally, clay should be stored in a damp atmosphere. If this is not possible, the polythene bags in which it is sold will keep the contents moist for several months provided the bag is not punctured. Plastic bins and buckets with lids are useful for storing clay that has been wedged.

For keeping unfinished work moist between sessions, wrap the piece well in cling film or polythene and place it away from heat or direct sunlight.

Lots of shelf space is invaluable in a studio, particularly for doing runs of work. Movable planks resting on wall brackets rather than fixed shelves are also a good idea. This way you can bring the shelf to where you are working rather than carrying individual pieces to the shelf.

Unlike clay, which should be kept damp, dry ingredients are best kept in a dry place. Plastic storage jars and bins are excellent for this. Mixed glazes can also be stored in bins and buckets, provided they have well-fitting lids. Dry ceramic ingredients can look remarkably similar, so make sure everything is well labelled. When storing glazes, include the recipe as well as the name or number of the glaze on the container.

THE WHIRLER

Certain projects in this book were made on a whirler, or banding wheel. This invaluable piece of equipment is a metal turntable, rather like a cake stand with a revolving top. Work done on a whirler can be turned constantly so that you can assess the piece from all sides. The whirler is also useful for applying bands of slip or glaze.

PLASTER SLABS

A plaster of Paris slab for reclaiming and drying out clay is invaluable. This is easy to make, to your own size and specifications. Make a simple mould using a smooth laminated board as the base and building up the sides of the mould with thick walls of clay slightly higher than the thickness of slab required. Press the clay firmly on to the board and join it at the corners to prevent the plaster from escaping.

Mix the plaster using approximately 4.5-5.5kg (10-12lbs) of plaster to 3.5 litres (8 pints) of water. This will make a slab approximately 25 x 25 x 8cm (10 x 10 x 3in). Start with the water in a large bucket, leaving plenty of room for the plaster. Sprinkle in the plaster without stirring, until the powder appears as little islands above the surface of the water. Leave for a few moments, then stir well to get rid of any lumps, keeping your hands below the water to avoid creating bubbles.

When the plaster begins to thicken, pour about half of it into the mould. Lay a piece of hessian or open-weave fabric on the plaster for extra strength, then pour in the rest of the plaster. When the plaster has set, remove the clay walls and release the plaster by tapping the laminated base.

HEALTH AND SAFETY

Ceramics involves the use of potentially dangerous materials and equipment, and care should be taken at all times. Much of this is common sense, although some procedures - especially those involving the use of toxic chemicals - call for special precautions.

Here are some general guidelines for good health and safe practice in the home pottery:

• Do not drink, eat or smoke in the studio.
• Wash work surfaces after use, and wash hands after handling materials.
• Wear a mask for handling dry materials.
• Wear rubber or other protective gloves when handling glazes and other potentially dangerous materials.
• Wear overalls or work clothes made from nylon or another material that does not retain dust. Wash these regularly.
• Make sure the room is well ventilated.
• Cover all open cuts and sores.

HAZARDOUS MATERIALS

All materials should be handled with respect, but certain substances call for particular care. Be guided by the 'Harmful' and 'Toxic' labels on ceramic products, and follow the safety information in your supplier's catalogue.

Three essential pices of studio safety equipment - rubber gloves, safety goggles and a mask.

Only a few of the following are used in the projects in this book, but as a general guide the most potentially hazardous materials include: all lead compounds, antimony, barium carbonate, borax, boric acid, flint, quartz, on-glaze enamels, lustres, some under- and on-glaze colours, and some body and glaze stains.

The following materials are also toxic and require careful handling, as do any glazes containing them: cadmium, selenium, lithium, cobalt, copper oxide, copper carbonate, nickel oxide, chromium oxide, vanadium, nickel oxide, manganese dioxide, manganese carbonate, gold (mercury amalgam) and silver nitrate.

DUST AND DRY MATERIALS

Wear a mask whenever you are working with potentially harmful materials in powder form. Although some of these are not dangerous in themselves, inhaling or digesting any dusty substance is unhealthy and can cause

Dry materials are dangerous: whenever possible, damp down dry spills before cleaning up.

problems if it is breathed in over a period of time. Take special care when using any of the toxic materials listed above, and also when using sandpaper or an abrasive file on dry clay or biscuit ware.

Your ceramics supplier will advise you on selecting a mask. This may be a lightweight metal or fibre affair, or a more elaborate respirator-type mask which has two filters to make breathing easier. The latter is clumsier to wear, but may be advisable if you are sanding regularly or using other dust-making processes.

Finally, try to keep all dust to a minimum by cleaning up spills as soon as they occur – if glaze or clay is allowed to dry it becomes a health hazard. Wash all equipment and tools when wet. If possible, vacuum the studio floor; otherwise, damp down the dust with water before brushing.

GLAZE SAFETY

When using glazes, work in a well-ventilated room, preferably with an extractor fan. Avoid creating unnecessary dust by adding powdered ingredients to the water slowly, letting these slide into it without splashing. A mask is essential when mixing glazes, and it is also important to wipe up spilled materials and to wash your hands well as soon as you have finished. The silica - the glass-forming ingredient in a glaze - is particularly dangerous.

The glazed projects in this book are either dipped or painted. However, larger objects can also be sprayed, in which case you should wear an appropriate mask. Spraying should be done in the open air or in a special spray booth, preferably with a built-in extractor.

KILN SAFETY

Make sure your kiln is properly installed and regularly maintained. Many ceramic substances, including lustre glazes, give off poisonous fumes when fired, so the room should be well ventilated, preferably with an extractor. Various venting and air-extraction systems are available, depending on the size and type of kiln, so ask your manufacturer for advice.

Despite being well insulated, the outside of an electric kiln gets surprisingly hot and can cause nasty burns. A wire cage, available from the supplier, is useful for preventing accidents; otherwise, keep people and pets well away from the kiln area.

Occasionally, you will need to look into a kiln through the viewing hole during firing. The intense light from a high firing can cause damage to the retina, so protect your eyes - preferably with special glasses.

CONTRIBUTING ARTISTS

Jacqui Atkin
10 Gower Road
Heaton Chapel
Stockport SK4 2QY
Tel 0161 432 0298

Rosie Bennell
16 Leagate Road
Heaton Moor
Stockport SK4 3NH
Tel 0161 432 0742

Maggie Angus Berkowitz
c/o Craft Potters Association
William Blake House
7 Marshall Street
London W1V 1LP

Kirsti Buhler Fattorini
c/o Craft Potters Association
William Blake House
7 Marshall Street
London W1V 1LP

Geoff and Pat Fuller
The Three Stags' Heads
Wardlow Mires
Tideswell
Derbyshire SK17 8RW
Tel 01298 872268

Karin Hessenberg
c/o Craft Potters Association
William Blake House
7 Marshall Street
London W1V 1LP
and
The Crafts Council
44A Pentonville Road
London N1 9BY

Syl Macro
Stokoe House Gallery
Market Place
Alston
Cumbria CA9 3HS
Tel 01434 382137

Sarah Perry
51 Annandale Road
Greenwich
London SE10 0DE
Tel 0181 858 2665

Paul Scott
Email:
paulscott@dial.pipex.com

Polly and Garry Uttley
Chesterfield
Tel/fax 01246 824797

Josie Walter
c/o Craft Potters Association
William Blake House
7 Marshall Street
London W1V 1LP

SUPPLIERS OF CERAMIC MATERIALS

UK
Potclays Ltd
Brickkiln Lane
Etruria
Stoke-on-Trent ST4 7PB

Bath Potter Supplies
2 Dorset Close
Bath BA2 3RF

Potterycrafts Ltd
Campbell Road
Stoke-on-Trent ST4 4ET

Spencroft Ceramics Ltd
Spencroft Road
Holditch Industrial estate
Newcastle-upon-Tyne ST5 7BP

Sneyd Oxides Ltd
Sneyd Mills
Leonora Street
Burslem
Stoke-on-Trent ST6 3BZ

The Potters Connection Ltd
Longton Mill
Anchor Road
Longton ST3 1JW

USA
**Ceramic Supply of New
York and New Jersey**
7 Route 46 West
Lodi
NJ 07644

Continental Clay Company
1101 Stenson Boulevard NE
Minneapolis
Min 55413

ART Studio Clay Company
4717 West 16th Street
Indianapolis
Indiana 46222

**Del-Val Potters Supply
Company**
7600 Queen Street
Wyndmoor
PA 19118

Ferro Corporation
PO Box 6650
Cleveland
Ohio 44101

Randall Pottery Inc.
Box 774
Alfred
New York 14802

ACKNOWLEDGEMENTS

The author would like to thank all the artists who have contributed to this book. Thanks are also due to the following:

Potclays Limited, for help with the materials and equipment on pages 16–17, for the photographs and products on pages 20, 21 and 28, and for the photographs on pages 34–35.

Barbara Blenkinship (Tel 0176 888 649), author of *Wetheriggs Pottery: A History and Collector's Guide* (Spencer Publications 1988).

Ian and Lesley Howes; Adrian Smith; Fiona Eaton, Alison Myer and Sarah Widdicombe at David & Charles.

For the loan of pots and photographs in the Gallery pages: Jacqui Atkin, Barbara Blenkinship, Geoff Fuller, Pat Fuller, Karin Hessenberg, Sarah Perry.

GLOSSARY

Alumina Essential ingredient in almost every glaze, which helps to harden and stabilize it. Sometimes known as the amphoteric.

Ball clay Strong, fine-particled clay which has high plasticity.

Biscuit-ware Unglazed, usually porous pots which have been fired once to make them more sturdy for glazing. Sometimes known as bisque-ware.

Bisque-ware See Biscuit-ware.

Bone china Tough, translucent white clay which contains calcined bone ash and china clay. Bone china has low plasticity and for this reason is usually used for slip casting.

Bow harp Metal or wooden harp with a taut wire used for cutting clay. Most harps now have an adjustable wire.

Casting slip Slip used in a mould to produce slipware. Casting slip usually contains a deflocculant to help disperse the clay particles evenly in the liquid.

China clay An extremely white clay with low plasticity, used in clay bodies and glazes. Also known as kaolin.

Crazing Fine cracks on the glazed surface, often caused by different degrees of shrinkage between the clay body and the glaze.

Fettling Removal of drips of glaze and unwanted glaze from the base of pots. Also used to describe the trimming of a leather-hard pot.

Flux Glaze ingredient which lowers or modifies the melting or maturing point of the glaze.

Frit Powdered glaze ingredient, produced by melting lead or other toxic material with silica to render the toxic material less harmful. The glass-like substance is then ground to a fine powder.

Glaze Glass-like coating fused on to the surface of a clay vessel.

Green glazing See Once firing.

Grog Ground biscuit-ware used in clay bodies to add texture and increase firing strength.

Kidney Kidney-shaped tool used for shaping and scraping clay.

Kiln High-firing oven used by potters. Kilns may be run by electricity, gas, propane, wood, coal or oil.

Kneading Final process used in the preparation of clay, which is similar to kneading dough.

Leather hard Clay which has dried until it is the texture of leather – it is still damp, but has lost its flexibility.

Lustre Metallic or iridescent glaze which is applied and fired on to an already glazed pot.

Molochite Fired, ground china clay used as a grog in white clay bodies such as porcelain.

Mould Plaster or biscuit form used for shaping plastic clay or slip.

On-glaze colours Decorative colours applied on top of a fired glaze and fired to a lower temperature.

Once firing Glaze firing a pot which has not been biscuit fired. Also known as raw glazing or green glazing.

Oxides Elements which have been combined with oxygen. Copper, cobalt and other oxides are used for colouring glazes, slips and clay bodies.

Oxidized firing Firing in which enough oxygen is allowed into the kiln to ensure the glaze colours remain unaffected. See also Reduction firing.

Plasticity The degree to which wet clay can be worked and moulded without flaking or cracking.

Porcelain High-firing, translucent white clay made from china clay, feldspar and flint or quartz.

Primary clay Clay which has remained at the site of its formation.

Raku Firing technique in which the pots are heated rapidly and then removed hot from the kiln. They are then usually placed in sawdust or other combustible materials to produce local reduction on the glaze colours.

Reduction firing Process in which the kiln is starved of oxygen during firing, causing the oxygen atoms in the colouring oxides to be burned up. The process produces characteristic 'reduced' colours.

Scoring Roughening or cutting the edges of clay, usually before wetting or slipping and joining.

Secondary clay Clay which has been carried from the site of its formation by land movement, glaciers, water or wind.

Sgrafitto Decoration made by scratching into the surface of the clay or glaze, often to reveal the colour or colours underneath.

Silica Main glass-forming material in a glaze.

Slip Clay mixed with water to a smooth, creamy consistency and used for decoration.

Smoke firing Decorating a clay body or glaze by firing in sawdust, newspaper or other combustible material.

Spiral wedging Symmetrical type of kneading used mainly in the preparation of largish lumps of clay.

T-material Highly plastic and refractory clay body containing molochite. It is particularly resistant to thermal shock (sudden changes of temperature).

Underglaze colours Decorating colours which are applied to wet or leather-hard clay or biscuit-ware, and then glazed.

Wedging Initial process in the preparation of clay, in which the clay is cut in two and the pieces turned and then slammed together repeatedly in order to mix the clay.

INDEX